STRUCTURING A LEARNER-CENTERED SCHOOL

by

Linda Schrenko

IRI/Skylight Publishing, Inc.
Palatine, Illinois

LB
2805
S426
1994

Structuring a Learner-Centered School
Second Printing

Published by IRI/Skylight Publishing, Inc.
200 E. Wood Street, Suite 274
Palatine, Illinois 60067
Phone 800-348-4474, 708-991-6300
Fax 708-991-6420

Creative Director: Robin Fogarty
Editors: Carolyn Hogan, Julia E. Noblitt, Heidi Ray
Type Compositor: Donna Ramirez
Book Designers: Bruce Leckie, David Stockman
Production Coordinator: Amy Behrens

Library of Congress Catalog Card Number 94-75255

Printed in the United States of America.

ISBN 0-932935-74-5

1005B-2-95

Acknowledgments

Thanks to Roslyn Brown, Director of the Effective Teaching Program, New York State United Teachers, and the instruction team of Eleanor Wereley, Neil Rothman, Ann Rosen, Bill Ferris, Barbara Egan, Cathy Chester, Annette Truby, Linda Kantor, and Ida Quade.

Contents

The learner-centered school

America 2000, *A New Compact for Learning*, charter schools, restructuring, authentic assessment, cooperative learning . . . the list of educational "happenings" could go on indefinitely. Educational reform (restructuring, renewal, resizing) is being enacted around the world, as an increasing number of schools in the United States, Canada, and Europe are exploring learner-centered structures. In New York State, the major state-mandated restructuring plan, *A New Compact for Learning*, identifies the learner-centered classroom as a major goal.

But what do we mean by the term *learner-centered?* And didn't we try this approach back in the 1960s? What became of it? Why is it being discussed again? The answers to these questions will vary from person to person, state to state, and even researcher to researcher.

IRI/Skylight Publishing, Inc.

*Your
Ideas*

The concept of the learner-centered school is not new. In John Dewey's *Democracy and Education* (1916), a lab school is described as a plan for education with no discrete grades and much emphasis on "cooperative social organization." The Dewey lab school focused on the students' needs rather than on covering a well-defined scope and sequence of curriculum. Much of Dewey's philosophy is evident in the learner-centered classroom. Students become a part of a learning team, empowered to make choices and to move at their own pace. This learner-centered type of education prevailed throughout the early schools, until the onset of the industrial revolution changed America's vision of education.

Schools moved away from Dewey's concepts and embraced the industrial or factory system of education introduced in the United States by Horace Mann. In the "factory" school, all students are grouped chronologically, taught the same material from the same textbook, and expected to function in an obedient, nonquestioning manner. This system was intended to prepare all students in the same way and to ready them for work on an assembly line. At one time, this system was useful, but in today's world, computers and robots do much of the dull, routine assembly-line work that was previously delegated to factory workers. Today's students must be able to think, to make decisions, to transfer knowledge, to acquire new skills, and to work together in teams. The old method simply does not work anymore. In fact, some argue it probably never worked.

Prior to the industrial revolution, education was carried out either by private tutoring or in mixed-age groups (e.g., the one-room school). Older students were expected to help younger classmates, and a spirit of cooperation, caring, and teamwork was the philosophy of most schools. These early attempts at educating the whole child were much more in line with learner-centered instruction than the factory system developed in the latter part of the twentieth century.

IRI/Skylight Publishing, Inc.

The advent of the industrial revolution created a need for education of the masses. Mann's assembly-line model spread throughout the United States. With the 1957 launch of Sputnik, America awoke to find itself behind other nations in academics. This prompted a reexamination of policies and practices. Learner-centered concepts were reintroduced in the schools. And then, like so many other educational practices, they disappeared.

Your Ideas

It was not until the early 1980s that the American educational system saw the need to address increased criticism. Many blamed teachers, and some blamed administrators. Researchers debated statistics that contrasted perceptions of the performance of students in past decades with that of the present. As a result, many Band-Aids and quick fixes were mandated by legislatures, but they failed to accomplish the goal of a quality education for all children. Those failures and the country's continued frustration with schools gave birth to a new notion: the system needed to be reformed.

By the 1990s, the call for systemic change led people to question the basic principles and practices of the traditional model. There was now an interest in returning to the learner-centered concept. However, it was not until the American Psychological Association produced a concise, research-based summary of the basic principles of learner-centered schooling, that a concise framework for defining the nature of a learner-centered school emerged (Alexander & Murphy, 1993).

The panel agreed on twelve learner-centered psychological principles that define the learner and the learning process in the context of environmental conditions conducive to learning. From these principles sprang the many practices, structures, and processes that are the foundation of the new conception of learner-centered schooling. They provide new impetus for designing approaches to schooling that will most enable learners to succeed. Following are the learner-centered principles:

IRI/Skylight Publishing, Inc.

*Your
Ideas*

Principle 1. *The nature of the learning process.* Learning is a natural process of discovering and constructing meaning from information and experience filtered through each learner's unique perceptions, thoughts, and feelings.

Principle 2. *The goals of the learning process.* Each learner seeks to create an understanding of acquired data, revise it, and make it understandable to others.

Principle 3. *The construction of knowledge.* Each learner makes unique links of new and old knowledge in order to construct deeper understanding.

Principle 4. *Metacognition.* When learners plan, monitor, and assess how they think, they develop expertise and critical and creative thought.

Principle 5. *Motivation influences learning.* A learner's locus of control, sense of responsibility, goals, interests, competence, and expectations feed an individual's motivation to succeed.

Principle 6. *Intrinsic motivation to learn.* Each learner has a natural propensity to learn. When this is thwarted by negative experiences, learning becomes difficult.

Principle 7. *Characteristics of motivation-enhancing learning tasks.* When provided with authentic learning tasks that challenge curiosity, creativity, and complex thinking, the learner is motivated to engage in increasingly difficult learning tasks.

Principle 8. *Developmental nature of learning.* Each individual progresses through the stages of development at different times.

Principle 9. *Social and cultural diversity.* Learning is facilitated by interacting with individuals of diverse backgrounds, interests, and values.

Principle 10. *Positive relationships.* Learning is enhanced when learners experience quality relationships that provide support and show care and respect.

Principle 11. *Individual differences.* Each learner, shaped by a combination of inherited genes and environmental factors, has different capabilities, preferences, and propensities for learning.

Principle 12. *Cognitive filters.* Each learner processes new ideas through the filters of belief, understanding, interpretations, and attitudes, which create unique constructions of meaning. (Alexander & Murphy, 1993)

IRI/Skylight Publishing, Inc.

1

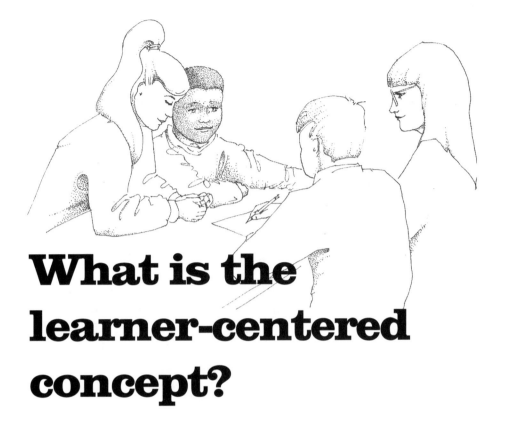

What is the learner-centered concept?

When educators use the term *learner-centered*, what do they mean? Many think of learner-centered instruction as the use of learning centers for a theme, topic, or subject, such as math or art. Others think of alternative types of assessment where students are evaluated in nontraditional ways. Still others think of continuous progress models, integrated thematic instruction, and cooperative learning. In truth, learner-centered education is all of these things and more. When planning a learner-centered school, it is important that teachers, administrators, parents, and students converse about the different concepts of learner-centered instruction and develop a common vocabulary that facilitates its creation.

IRI/Skylight Publishing, Inc.

Your Ideas

In defining *learner-centered*, it may be helpful to look back at how each of us learned to extrapolate the generic qualities that made school a good experience.

Think of a time

Think of a time when you learned something quickly, easily, and well. Use the web below to jot down a description of one or two instances of learning that have left a lasting impression on you. Review your experiences.

1. What do these experiences have in common?
2. Where were you?
3. Who were you with?
4. How did you feel?

Web

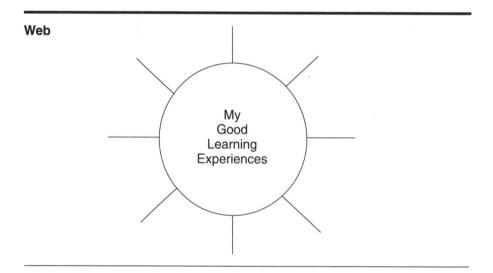

My Good Learning Experiences

Look over your web and see how it meets with the following "high points."

"I was interested in the concept to be learned."

A person's interest in a topic or an activity will create intrinsic motivation. This motivation will translate into more thought, effort, and time spent on the topic or activity. Thus, learning is increased. Learner-centered schools promote each child's internal motivation; these schools shy away from extrinsic motivation and forcing all students to fit a pattern.

IRI/Skylight Publishing, Inc.

"Someone modeled the behavior or skill for me."
Frequently we learn best, not by hearing about a concept, but by first seeing someone demonstrate the behavior we are to learn. For example, a math teacher might do a long division problem on the board, saying his or her thought process aloud so that students see and hear the procedure to solve the problem. By modeling the desired behavior, the teacher allows students to experience the learning in a more relevant manner, making it easier to learn and remember. In learner-centered schools, teachers use proven instructional practices, such as modeling, asking higher-order questions, and mediating student thought.

"I was engaged in hands-on, meaningful experiences."
This is one of the most popular responses. Unfortunately, many times such direct experiences are not possible for students. However, when a teacher can provide many simulations of real-life experiences and varied opportunities to solve hands-on problems for abstract concepts, students will learn. In the learner-centered school, hands-on problem solving is the norm, not the exception.

"I received constructive feedback."
Feedback that is threatening, negative, or demeaning does not increase learning. Feedback given in a positive, coaching manner is most effective. The skillful coach gives feedback by modeling, by encouraging, and by allowing students multiple opportunities to practice and improve the desired learning. In the learner-centered school, student assessment is geared to helping each student improve learning. Feedback on what to improve is critical.

"Emotion was attached to my best learning."
Generally speaking, the stronger the emotion associated with a learning task, the stronger the learning. For

Your Ideas

example, many of us can remember in great detail the sequence of events that occurred at the funeral of a loved one. We do not need drill or practice for our long-term memory to be accessed. The power of the emotion makes long-term retention of this event highly likely. But negative emotion is not the only creator of learning. Many people remember vividly a special Christmas, a birth, or a wedding. Either positive or negative emotion affects learning—it is the strength of the emotion that determines the depth of the learning. In the learner-centered school, teachers search for those emotion-filled projects that will excite the student.

"I had to think."
Since research has shown that the brain *seeks* patterns, it is important for the learner-centered teacher to provide opportunities for students to see patterns and perhaps create their own.

What are the belief systems that support the learner-centered school?

The learner-centered school is one in which many of the criteria listed above are present most of the time in all classrooms. These criteria are the core around which learner-centered teachers build each day's instruction. They build an underlying belief system about how schools and teachers can best stimulate learning.

All children come to school willing and able to learn.

For many schools, that statement has become the central driving belief in the school mission. Yet, some individual educators do not believe that all children can learn. Others don't accept that all students come to school willing to learn. Thus, the statement becomes a handy catch phrase, a conversation topic that is unrelated to actual belief about children's potential.

A growing body of research proves the value of practices that promote this belief. Cognitive psychologists and researchers, such as Robert Sternberg, Barbara Presseisen, Rueven Feuerstein, and many others, have demonstrated that all children do have the potential to learn whatever the school is ready to teach. Feuerstein's successful work with students labeled retarded, emotionally disturbed, or gifted underachievers has demonstrated time and time again what true belief in the learning potential of even the most challenged child paired with correct methodology can accomplish.

Many learner-centered teachers' classroom experiences support the research. They trust that if they provide appropriate instruction for students, then their students can and will learn. These beliefs create a learning environment where all students can learn.

All intelligence is modifiable.

When Binet and Weschler introduced the concept of measuring intelligence, it was assumed that intelligence was a fixed entity from birth, could be quantified, and was unchangeable. In more recent years, Piaget, Vygotsky, Feuerstein, and others have come to believe through their long-term observations of children that intelligence is *not* fixed.

Intelligence is formed by a combination of genetic predispositions, experiences, and environment. Teachers and parents can modify intelligence by modifying the climate and the instruction they provide the child. Bad environment and bad instruction can decrease intelligence; good environment and good instruction can increase intelligence.

Feuerstein's work carries the principle of cognitive modifiability another step. His *Instrumental Enrichment* program, used in seventy countries, and the *Learning*

Your Ideas

*Your
Ideas*

Potential Assessment Device are world-recognized approaches that help learner-centered teachers mediate learning and modify intelligence. Howard Gardner in his Project Zero research at Harvard has developed a theory that reinforces Feuerstein. Gardner's theory details seven intelligences that are changeable: bodily/kinesthetic, verbal/linguistic, visual/spatial, mathematical/logical, musical/rhythmic, interpersonal, and intrapersonal. Gardner believes that everyone has predispositions toward some of these intelligences, that each child possesses all of the intelligences to some degree, and that anyone can expand an intelligence.

Teachers *enable* learning by creating conditions for learning by all.

If a teacher believes that all children can learn, then it becomes his or her challenge to provide meaningful experiences that will lead to learning. It is not sufficient for teachers to teach to the middle of the class or to "dump" information in long lectures. When the teacher teaches to the middle students, he or she misses the top one-third of the students as well as the bottom one-third. Two-thirds of the class are not learning! For the teacher who believes all children can learn, this is an unacceptable situation. The teacher's challenge, then, is to provide a variety of experiences on different levels to enable every child to stretch his or her potential. Varied activities, meaningful experiences, thoughtful reflection, discovery learning centers, and other student-focused activities enable the teacher to help every child become a successful learner.

When teachers spend most of their time lecturing to students, Sternberg (1986) points out that it's the teachers themselves who are getting smarter. Whether in high school or kindergarten, learner-centered students cannot be passive receptacles into which facts and figures are dumped. The learner-centered teacher structures emotion-filled, hands-on activities that make children think and talk about *their* ideas.

IRI/Skylight Publishing, Inc.

Using mindful approaches, learner-centered teachers mediate learning *by all.*

The teacher who creates optimal conditions for learning, becomes a *facilitator* of learning rather than a dumper of information. The teacher who is trained to help students develop individual thinking and problem- solving potential and who intervenes in the student's thinking processes becomes a *mediator* of learning. Building on Feuerstein's (1980) and Vygotsky's (1986) work, Presseisen (1986) and others have focused on the power of mediation and socially shared cognition as critical elements for advancing student learning. The cognitive mediator is a teacher with advanced skills who enables students to strengthen their patterns of thinking and construct new understandings about important problems, concepts, and issues by intervening in the student's thought processes.

In the past decade, cognitive psychologists have studied the thinking that students do to plan, monitor and evaluate their learning tasks. More and more, these researchers argue that the "thinking about thinking" approach is a critical determinant of any increases in student achievement. Using the term "metacognition," the "thinking one does about the act of thinking," researchers, such as Anne Brown and Anne Marie Palincsar (1982), and Beau Fly Jones (1987), also have noted that it is important for the classroom teacher to assist students in planning and evaluating the thinking processes that they use to gather information, problem-solve, and make decisions. Brown and her colleagues' (1981) studies show the powerful impact of metacognition for advancing students' reading abilities. Arthur Whimbey (1975), the inventor of the paired-partner, problem-solving method, reinforces this notion for the field of mathematics.

Studies on metacognition have yielded a new, more precise description of the critical role a teacher plays in advancing student achievement through metacognitive

*Your
Ideas*

reflection (Fogarty, 1994). In this role, the teacher provides students with a learning task that requires higher-order critical, creative thinking skills. Rather than tell the students how to think through the task, the teacher uses questioning strategies, such as wait time, higher-order questions, and extending cues, detailed in the TESA* project, to enable the students to use inductive reasoning to understand and plan the thinking aspects of the learning task. Throughout the task, the teacher relies solely on questioning strategies to help the students use more precise thinking skills. At the end of the task, the teacher again resorts to inquiry, having students draw conclusions about the problem solving they just completed. In this sense, the teacher *stands between* or mediates the student and the thinking task and models the types of thinking and inquiring that the student can use to solve other unfamiliar but similar thinking tasks. Like the marriage counselor who stands between a disagreeing couple and assists them in resolving their disagreements, the teacher stands between the student and the thinking task to help the student solve the thoughtful problem. The teacher's role is called cognitive mediator.

In the learner-centered classroom, the mediation of cognition is very important. Not only does the teacher facilitate the learning task and ask the students to master the content of the course, he or she expects the students to think about what they are doing and to sharpen their thinking skills as they work. Ultimately, the teacher uses cognitive mediation skills to help each student to

---

*TESA (Teaching Expectations and Student Achievement) is a research project and training program. In the mid '70s, Samuel Kermin and his colleagues in the Los Angeles County Public Schools examined the differences in performance between high- and low-performing students. What they discovered was how teachers' different expectations of poor and minority students led to the use of instructional strategies that were different from the strategies used with middle-class, Caucasian students. To counter such "low-expectation instructional behaviors" as quick questioning, ignoring, and fact questioning that they found targeted at the poor and minority students, the researchers identified sixteen teaching behaviors that they associated with high-expectation teaching. They hypothesized and later proved that use of these high-expectation teaching behaviors with all children, especially with poor and minority students, would make significant differences in the students' achievement. Today, this highly successful training program is offered nationally by the Phi Delta Kappa National Dissemination Center and is a part of many teacher training programs on critical thinking.

IRI/Skylight Publishing, Inc.

understand his or her thinking style and to individualize his or her personal best approach to thinking and problem solving.

Your Ideas

Facilitator vs. Mediator

A *facilitator* of learning is a teacher who structures the learning environment with interactive learning tasks to make learning for all students successful. (Facilitate comes from the Latin word *Facile*, which translates into *easily*.) A *mediator* of learning is a teacher trained to assist students in increasing their abilities to process cognitive tasks and to apply new cognitive skills in a variety of learning tasks.

Learning best occurs when individuals construct their own meaning.

The brain is a pattern-seeking device (Hart, 1975). When it fails to find a pattern or meaning, the learning that occurs is short-term and quickly forgotten. When students memorize information in order to pass a test, nearly 80 percent of the knowledge is lost within two weeks.

The learner-centered school operates on active learning principles such as those promulgated by Vygotsky (1986):

1. Learners create knowledge through personal experiences.
2. Learners create knowledge through personal experiences with others.
3. Learners create knowledge by sharing experiences with others.
4. Learners create knowledge through collaborative interactions with others.

Note how Vygotsky accentuates the phrase, "Learners *create*. . . ." This "sine qua non," translates into instructional practices appropriate for learner-centered classrooms, as follows:

1. If teachers are to maximize student learning, they must help students *build on prior knowledge*. Every

student comes to the learning situation with prior experiences and prior knowledge.

Teachers who use this prior knowledge as a bridge help the student to construct meaning and make long-term retention more likely. For example, a child who is learning to divide can easily relate to the experience of sharing cookies in equal parts with two, three, four, or more friends. From there it is a simple leap to the concept of division, because the child sees the need and practical value of the topic.

2. Teachers can help students learn when they assist the student *make sense of the learning*. Students must make connections to prior learning or other similar situations for the new learning to make sense. The teacher facilitates this new learning by providing projects or experiences that make it possible for each child to see relationships and connect concepts.

In addition, the teacher can mediate the students' cognitive development by processing not only the new information, but the thinking needed to form new patterns. For example, a child experimenting with cracking eggs begins to see a pattern after a number of trials. He or she may generalize from the pattern that all eggs have yolks. By *mediating* the discovery through questions, the teacher helps the child make fundamental connections, and the child learns that all eggs have similar properties.

3. For students to learn best, they *must learn how to think*. As the teacher structures learning experiences, he or she teaches students to use questioning strategies, critical thinking skills, processing strategies, graphic organizers, and reflective thinking to give them the necessary tools to meet future challenges. A simple way to create a more thoughtful classroom is to have a student tell a partner one thing he or she remembers from a lesson or one thing that surprised him or her. This not only adds more reflection, it

IRI/Skylight Publishing, Inc.

keeps students attentive and thinking during the lesson. Beyond this think-pair-share, there are a multitude of strategies and programs which enhance thinking by all students (Bellanca and Fogarty, 1986).

Students must learn *to work in teams.*

Over five hundred studies demonstrate the value of learning in cooperative groups versus competitive and isolated activities. Note the prominent role of shared experience in Vygotsky's principles on page 10. Businesses tell the schools that their first priority is to have employees who can think and work as a team. Research tells us that thinking skills can best be acquired and applied in cooperative groups (Bellanca and Fogarty, 1986). Teachers also find that students are much more willing to engage in difficult problem-solving tasks when they work in groups rather than as individuals. The support and responsibility generated by belonging to a group enhances learning and creates a climate conducive to risk taking and increased learning.

In the constructivist framework, the value of cooperative learning goes a step beyond the need to learn teamwork. Constructivists assert that optimal learning conditions foster socially shared cognitions. During these interactions, students think together, mediating, debating, and synthesizing new insights. These interactions, aided by a skilled mediator, are critical in helping students learn how to learn.

Teachers facilitate learning by using different pacing and by recognizing multiple pathways to learning.

To assume that all six-year-olds will learn a concept the same way is as ridiculous as assuming that all six-year-olds will wear the same size shoes and clothes. It may sound good in theory, but it does not work in the diverse

*Your
Ideas*

world where we live. Some educational theorists have defended didactic, rote teaching as being "fair" to all students. It is hardly that! It is imperative that all who enter teaching realize that every child is unique and should be treated accordingly. Options such as continuous progress, mastery learning, and team teaching to meet the various needs of students should and must be considered.

Teachers also need a basic understanding of intelligence to help students learn best. Once again, to assume that all students learn the same way, understand the same way, or interpret the world in the same way is simplistic.

Cognitive research shows that students possess different kinds of minds and therefore learn and understand differently (Gardner, 1991). The evidence amassed by Howard Gardner of Harvard's Project Zero indicates that some students need a verbal/linguistic approach to learning while others favor logical/mathematical and still others visual/spatial. The teacher who understands the multiple intelligence theory can structure learning to meet the diverse needs of his or her students. According to Gardner, most learners benefit if material is presented in several different ways and learning is measured in several different ways (Gardner, 1983).

Learning occurs best when the school supports learner-centered instruction.

Goodlad and Anderson's model school (1987) places the student at the center of decision making. As curriculum, instruction, management, or support service issues surface in a school, decisions and their effect on students must receive first consideration. For instance, consider the lunch schedule issue in an elementary school whose population has exploded. The small lunchroom can no longer contain all the students at a noon sitting. The lunch staff needs one and a half hours of clean up time, but they don't want to stay on-site after 2:30 p.m. Therefore, the school decides to start the first lunch shift at 10:00 a.m. with "the little ones." The upper grades will eat at noon. This leaves time to clean up by 2:30 p.m.

In a learner-centered school, the effect of a 10:00 a.m. lunch on the students would be the first consideration. The kitchen staff's desire to leave by 2:30 p.m. would be considered after the most appropriate lunch times were set for students and teachers. A learner-centered school in California renegotiated the kitchen staff's union contract to allow for a longer workday ending at 4:00 p.m. Lunches were scheduled at 11:15 a.m., 12:00 p.m., and 12:45 p.m. until a second room could be prepared for a two-shift lunch period at 11:45 a.m. and 12:30 p.m.

Lunchroom schedules are not the only villain. In a Georgia high school, all students were dismissed on Fridays at 1:00 p.m. This allowed the bus company to transport students home before the buses were used to take teams and cheerleaders to games at 3:00 p.m. A more learner-centered arrangement would require moving Friday games to Saturday, with no shortening of the school day and no loss of instructional time.

If we look at the institution of school as a target, it is easy to see that there are many options for the center of the target. Each target center affects the way the school functions and the way teachers interact with students. If we look at several of the options, we can see the advantages and disadvantages that come with each possibility.

With the learner as the center of the target, instruction and assessment are built around the learner's needs. The schedule, school climate, facility, structure, and governance are all in tune to the learner's needs. Everyone in the school functions with the student as their reason for existence, and students' needs are the catalyst for all decisions made in the school.

Your Ideas

Your Ideas

The Learner-Centered Target

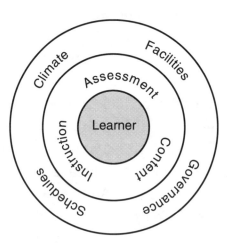

When the target center is changed to content, the reason for the school's existence becomes the delivery of content, which, in turn, affects the instruction, curriculum and assessment, content mandates, types of schedules, governance, facility needs, and student expectations. If focus is content, the student is expected to master the content regardless of its relevance to him or her.

The Content-Centered Target

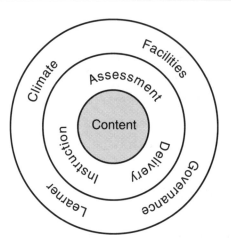

When bureaucracy runs the schools, the focus changes entirely. The institution serves to maintain the bureaucratic structures and positions. Instructional programs and assessment techniques are developed by a centralized bureaucracy that often has little contact with students or teachers. The governance becomes top-down, with schedules and facilities dictated from central "experts" who issue directives and set expectations with little knowledge of the students' needs. In fact, the bureaucracy's major concern is to find one size that fits every student.

The Bureaucracy-Centered Target

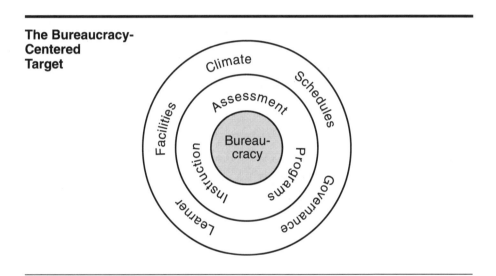

When athletic programs drive the school, the focus shifts away from instruction to maintaining the school's competitive teams. The schedules and facilities are shaped by the needs of the athletic programs and instruction and assessment are a distant second to the school's athletic programs (football, track, baseball, etc.). Athletes are often given preferential treatment, including the right to skip classes, receive larger lunch portions, go first in line, and wear special symbols of honor. Many are even recruited from other schools to ensure the dominance of the athletic program.

**The Athletic-
Centered
Target**

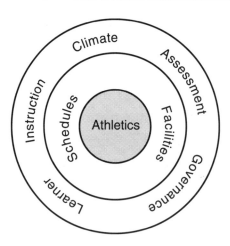

As strange as it may seem, auxiliary services can often become the central controlling factor in the school. When the lunchroom drives the school, the focus is entirely on conveniencing the cafeteria workers and their schedule. Students' schedules are designed around the lunchroom regardless of students' and teachers' needs. Collection of lunchroom money takes priority over instruction. Ensuring convenient flow of traffic in the lunchroom may cut short instructional periods. Everything is done to ensure that the food service workers' needs are met. Students are secondary.

**The Lunchroom-
Centered
Target***

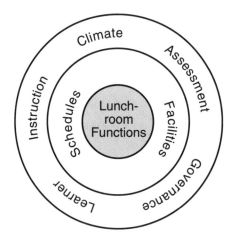

*May include bus drivers, custodians, or any school service area.

As is evident through examination of these targets, the entire focus of the school changes when the center of the target changes. True restructuring means putting the learners at the center of the educational target. Well-meaning district and school administrators and even teachers may find themselves missing the mark if they do not change their target focus to learner-centered.

Think about your school as it is today. What is your school's target?

Your School's Target

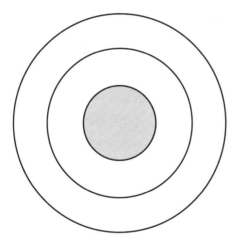

What would you prefer that target to be?

Your Preferred Target

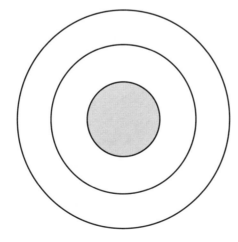

Your Ideas

What are the barriers to this change?

_____

_____

_____

_____

_____

_____

_____

_____

_____

_____

_____

_____

_____

_____

_____

_____

_____

_____

_____

_____

_____

_____

What do schools do to promote learner-centered classrooms?

The times are changing.

At the turn of the century, education was individualized, with many one-room schools and private tutors as the norm. The industrial revolution changed all of that. Employers wanted workers who were punctual, did not ask questions, and were capable of spending hours in monotonous jobs requiring rote memory. The schools set out to produce just such workers. Horace Mann visited and studied the Prussian military system of education that categorized all children of like chronological age into groups. These groups were pushed through a predetermined "assembly-line" curriculum, enabling large numbers to learn reading, writing, and arithmetic. This assembly-line approach seemed just what industrial America needed. The factory system caught on in the

IRI/Skylight Publishing, Inc.

U.S. and continues almost unchallenged today as the basic way to organize learning.

As the twenty-first century approaches, learner-centered advocates are calling for systemic change. Such change begins with a review of the systemic elements of the factory system. Such a review shows how the "pieces" fit the whole and what new "pieces" are needed to fit the new learner-centered system.

The systemic challenge

Breaking away from the traditional structure of schools to the learner-centered structure is a systemic challenge. Individuals and groups greet the challenge with varying degrees of enthusiasm. Some teachers become alarmed because they are moving outside their comfort zones into uncharted territory. Because the experience of the learner-centered classroom is unfamiliar, some teachers and administrators may tend to hang on to the status quo. As with any new endeavor, there will be rough spots and problems with curriculum, instruction scheduling, and parents. Those who do not understand the change process may feel insecure with the new elements. Therefore, providing a school climate that is comfortable enough for teachers to be willing to take risks and try new ideas becomes crucial to success.

A teacher accustomed to discrete grade levels, textbook-driven curriculum, and top-down management, may find the concept of the learner-centered classroom overwhelming. Studies show that in the learner-centered classroom as well as the traditional classroom, the most important variable for success is the teacher's skills and attitudes (Berliner and Casanova, 1993). Thus, to ensure that the learner-centered classroom has the maximum opportunity to succeed, the change process should begin with staff development. Teachers must have access to staff development that will enable them to understand the curriculum, teaching strategies, scheduling patterns, the change process, timelines for implementation of innovations, and other factors that will directly impact each classroom. They must also have time to discuss the new ideas, plan implementation of the new approaches, and revise their first attempts.

Typically, American policy makers have gone about the business of effecting change haphazardly. They have failed to understand that long-term change requires years of effort, massive amounts of staff development and support, and a commitment by those who will be most affected (i.e., students, teachers, and parents).

When a school system decides to implement a new program, the teachers responsible for the implementation often receive little or no training, sometimes only an hour or two of introduction and a copy of the text guidelines. They are left to struggle with the problem of implementation and must solve it with little ongoing support. At the end of the school year, many who tried unsuccessfully to implement new concepts not only return to their traditional programs, but develop an aversion to the innovation.

Systemic change

Systemic change requires cultural norms that promote collective action toward common goals (Williams, 1992). The action of the group as a unit rather than individuals within the group moves the system off dead center. As Peter Senge states, it is a "shift of mind" (1990). Systems thinking is now holistic and process-focused, as opposed to the traditional, fragmented scientific reasoning to which most of us are accustomed. It involves seeing the whole organization as a learning organization (Williams, 1992).

Senge (1990) defines the essential elements of the learning organization as:

- *Systems thinking*—a conceptual framework, a body of knowledge that makes patterns or relationships clear. Young children intuitively learn systems thinking.

Your Ideas

- *Personal mastery*—that special level of proficiency that allows us to clarify and deepen our personal vision, focus our energies, develop patience, and see reality.
- *Mental models*—our assumptions or generalizations that influence how we view the world and how we act.
- *Building shared vision*—a shared view of the future we strive to create. If it is genuine, people excel and learn because they want to rather than because they have to.
- *Team learning*—the ability of the group to engage in thinking together. Team learning is vital because teams, not individuals, are the fundamental learning unit in modern organizations.

As our society faces increasingly complex global problems, it becomes evident that the traditional scientific approach (i.e., the factory system of schooling) is inadequate to meet the needs of the school organization. Systems thinking more effectively deals with the larger, more complex problems of today's world. Senge believes that successful organizations must be able to adapt quickly to these changing conditions (Senge, 1990).

Despite the changing needs of society, most schools in the U.S. continue to operate in the factory system with its traditional assembly-line curriculum. What are the telling features of the factory school?

Mailbox curriculum

Content and skills are preset by bureaucrats and textbook manufacturers. The curriculum is often determined at the state level, with goals, objectives, and even activities and assessment set by state department personnel. In some states, such as New York and Indiana, the state assessment drives the curriculum. Often school action is shaped by the legislature or the governor's ideas of what education needs to be. Canned curriculum guides are

*Your
Ideas*

sent to local systems and taught to teachers in seminars and workshops. For example, the state of Georgia requires teachers to prove that they use the state-mandated Quality Core curriculum in their daily plans. State-level personnel then survey texts they believe will best support the curriculum. Of course, textbook publishers keep a careful eye on the state mandates and ensure that their texts are compatible so they can attract large orders. As a result, the curriculum looks like a rack of mailboxes in a post office. Every topic is slotted into a larger or smaller box depending on the state-mandated emphasis and is then assessed to make sure teachers have covered the required topics.

Behaviorist philosophy

Skinner's model for shaping behavior and teaching skills through reinforcement is the basis of assembly-line instruction. Repetition is the norm. The assumption is that children will respond and behave in the same way as laboratory rats.

Behaviorism is reflected most clearly in memory-based tests (Stimulus-response: Here are the facts; give them back.), fill-in-the-blanks/skill-drill workbooks, and direct instruction. Reward systems (stickers, smiley faces), punishments (detentions, paddles, expulsion from class), and grades are other popular behaviorist practices. These practices have many problems. Teachers have a difficult time financing these extrinsic rewards, and students begin to expect them for everything. Intrinsic motivation and self-satisfaction are weakened (Kohn, 1993).

Memorization

The traditional systems emphasizes rote memorization of facts to pass short-answer or multiple-choice tests. Little transfer of meaning is expected. Students learn information so that they may give it back to a teacher on a test.

*Your
Ideas*

Grades/grade point averages/class rank

Students are rank-ordered according to grade point average and rewarded with scholarships, honors, and acceptance by the best schools. Colleges look to GPAs to determine which students are accepted and which receive scholarships. Frequently, students take easy courses to have the best GPAs. Students quickly learn to "dummy down" their courses to raise GPAs and improve their class rank.

Tracking and ability grouping

Because this model stresses mass production, students who don't fit the norm are placed in different groups. Eventually they are tracked into different areas of study, eliminating the possibility for them to attend college or other advanced training. Some schools begin tracking as early as first grade. Students are placed in ability groups and the curriculum is either enriched (for the gifted) or "dummied down" (for the slow learner) to create appropriate levels for the students. Research tells us that neither gifted nor remedial students benefit from this practice (Oakes, 1985).

Schedules

In an assembly-line model, the schedule frames the instruction. Students lumped into ability groups rotate through forty- or fifty-minute segments of isolated study with no thought of integration or meaningfulness of instruction. Projects or research requiring more than a fifty-minute block of time are frequently abandoned, because they are too difficult for the teacher to manage. Much worthwhile learning is lost to the expediency of the bell.

Promotion and retention

Because of the discrete chronological segments corresponding to grade levels, the idea of promotion and reten-

IRI/Skylight Publishing, Inc.

Your Ideas

tion has gained support. If a student covers the curriculum, memorizes the facts, and recalls them for a test, he or she is promoted. Anyone who doesn't fit the narrow band of criteria is retained at that grade level an additional year. Regardless of mastery, after a student has been retained once, he or she is generally sent to the next grade level the following year. Occupying space for two consecutive years entitles the student to a promotion. Twelve or more years of sitting through classes entitles a student to a diploma. The skills and knowledge each student has at graduation will vary, but seat time is fixed.

Power and control via workbooks and lectures

In the factory system of education, teachers are the keepers of the knowledge. One of the teacher's primary functions is to give that knowledge or information to the students. The fastest and easiest method of disseminating information is for the teacher to lecture and the students to read and take notes. To ensure understanding, the student completes workbook pages designed by the textbook writers as follow-up activities. Though many teachers recognize the lecture method to be ineffective, they tend to return to the comfort zone of the traditional lecture and workbook classroom time and time again.

Individualized competition

In the factory school, the philosophy is every student for him- or herself. No collaboration is fostered in the schools. Students compete against each other rather than reaching for high personal standards. The bell curve creates an artificial competition. Even when the entire group is composed of honor students, using the bell curve means that only 20 percent can receive Bs and As and 20 percent must fail.

Your Ideas

Quick-fix inservice

In the factory system school, inservice is delivered from a central bureaucracy. Bureaucrats decide on the latest educational fad to be followed and mandate the change to the schools. They provide an "expert" to train teachers and administrators usually for one to two days and expect the teachers to fully implement the innovative techniques successfully. Generally, not even the central office staff has a full understanding of the innovation. With little or no follow-up support, the teachers who were "repaired" in the quick-fix program quickly revert to the comfort of the traditional practices they have performed for years. Between the lack of support activities, such as peer coaching, principals who are biased toward old methods, and the knowledge that this fad too will pass, is it any wonder that so many teachers greet new innovations with concern?

Hierarchical organization

Just as factories were organized on the hierarchical framework with authority flowing down from top to bottom, schools in the factory system are organized so that decisions are made at the top by a superintendent (district) and by a principal (school) and passed down for implementation by teachers and other "subordinant" staff.

In the hierarchical organization, authority is granted by position. The highest authority, the superintendent, has the power to make and enforce policy throughout the system. Even when the school system allows committees, the decision-making power is granted by the hierarchy.

Hierarchial Organization

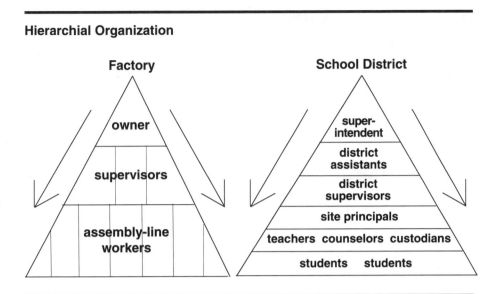

Supervision and leadership

In the hierarchial model, teachers and special services personnel are at the bottom. The administrators in the hierarchy strive to ensure that those under their authority implement the district's policies and procedures. For the classroom teacher, this translates to teaching the curriculum, maintaining classroom order, protecting the property, ensuring safety, and performing such other duties as assigned. The administrator evaluates annual performance to ensure that teachers carry out their duties. Evaluation includes classroom observations of instruction, completion of an observation check list and, a follow-up conference. The administrator files a report on the instructional performance. If the performance is not satisfactory, the teacher may be "remediated."

Learner-centered reaction

The learner-centered system is a natural reaction to the factory system. It is generated by the teachers, students, and administrators who have seen the fallacies of the traditional system and want to implement an educational system that will make a difference. Certain characteristics are evident in the learner-centered school.

A focus on performance

Contrary to the factory system which focuses on test scores and grades, the learner-centered school centers on thoughtful expectations and high standards. *School* is defined in terms of the *performance* desired by the local community and the results obtained by the students.

Developmentally appropriate practice

The learner-centered school or classroom focuses on the success of all students. In the traditional classroom, children at six years of age are expected to know and do the same things. In a learner-centered classroom, developmentally appropriate activities are designed to help students use the thinking and learning strategies they will need to succeed both in school and in life. For example, students in kindergarten and first grade are *not asked* to sit and perform paper-and-pencil tasks all day. They are allowed to explore and discover inductively in centers designed for learning.

In a learner-centered system, standards are established, and each child is expected to achieve those standards. The time required to master skills may vary, but the standards do not. All students are expected to learn and to develop to their fullest potential.

Authentic experiences

Learner-centered classrooms focus on meaningful experiences. Learner-centered teachers know that a "being there" experience is the best type of teaching; so they provide as many real experiences as possible. If a "being there" experience is not possible, the teacher provides a hands-on simulation to allow students to experience as much first-hand knowledge as possible. For example, a middle school teacher, when studying pond ecology, created a pond in her room. Students observed and studied the "pond" filled with plants, turtles, tadpoles, and other pond animals. Because daily visits to a real pond site were unavailable, a pond site was simulated in the classroom pool.

Your Ideas

Performance assessment

In the learner-centered classroom, assessment is as real as instruction. Rather than short-answer or multiple-choice tests that measure rote memorization, the learner-centered classroom teacher assesses a student's actual performance. Through projects, plays, presentations, or portfolio items, the teacher observes the student's mastery of concepts through actual performance of the skills. For example, high school students may conduct a research project, write a report, and deliver an oral presentation with visual aids. All teachers can be present to ask questions and to evaluate performance in science, social studies, math, language arts (both oral and written), organization, knowledge of content, and other areas pertinent to the project or presentation.

Flexible time

Scheduling in the learner-centered classroom also differs from the traditional classroom. Students do not change subjects mechanically every forty or fifty minutes with no thought of integration or continuity. They follow flexible schedules that integrate subjects, enabling depth of study as well as breadth. For instance, in one middle school, students are scheduled with a team of three teachers for a four-hour block of time labeled "Academics." These teachers are free to team-teach, to use all four hours for one subject, to group flexibly, etc. In other words, they use the time in the ways they believe best meet the needs of their students.

Primary examples of learner-centered scheduling

One learner-centered option effective at the primary level is the multiage, continuous-progress model. Used in

Your Ideas

many Canadian and British schools, the multiage concept is based on the one-room school of the 1800s. Students are placed in clusters or "families" based not on chronological age, but on development level. Children of different ages (usually no more than a three-year span) are grouped heterogeneously and allowed to move at their own pace through a curriculum or series of skills to be mastered before moving to the next group. Students move as rapidly or slowly as their need dictates—often spending two to three years with the same teacher or team of teachers. Flexible grouping allows students of different ages to work together based on similar interests, skills, or needs. Students do not fail if they progress more slowly; they simply remain with the group longer.

Primary Multiage: Sample Schedule I

Time	Activity
8:00–8:45 A.M.	Arrival. Free choice of language arts activities—journals, independent reading, seminar (help sessions), peer reading, listening, writing table, project work, learning centers
8:45–9:00 A.M.	Transition to whole group—completion/cleanup activities
9:00–10:00 A.M.	Shared reading—read to, read by, read with teacher
10:00–10:30 A.M.	Creative movement/P.E./musical activities
10:30–10:45 A.M.	Break (snacks, outside in good weather)
10:45–11:45 A.M.	Writing—total group instruction on some portion of the writing process (prewriting, mechanics, usage, editing) Individual/group writing—language experience, peer editing. Shared writing experiences—peer share/total group share
11:45 A.M.–12:00 P.M.	Teacher's choice—read to students
12:00–12:30 P.M.	Lunch
12:30–1:30 P.M.	Math centers—manipulatives, whole group instruction, problem solving, story problems, puzzles, shared math Reflection on math learning
1:30–1:50 P.M.	Recess
1:50–2:50 P.M.	Thematic unit activities—shared reading, content reading, projects, independent work
2:50–3:00 P.M.	Reflection on day's work

Primary Multiage: Sample Schedule II

8:15–8:30 A.M.	Opening/calendar
8:30–8:40 A.M.	Silent/independent reading
8:40–9:20 A.M.	Language experience and centers
9:20–9:55 A.M.	Exploratory (music, P.E., etc.)
9:55–10:10 A.M.	Recess
10:10–10:55 A.M.	Centers (integrated subjects)
10:55–11:55 A.M.	Math
11:55 A.M.–12:45 P.M.	Lunch
12:45–1:00 P.M.	Read aloud
1:00–2:00 P.M.	Reading activities
2:00–2:20 P.M.	Reflection
2:20 P.M.	Dismissal

Middle school examples of learner-centered scheduling

A middle school example of learner-centeredness might be the use of Feuerstein's *Instrumental Enrichment* program for the sixth-, seventh-, and eighth-grade students. Students are given explicit instruction two and a half hours per week in cognitive strategies and thinking skills, which are then used in their other subject areas. Teachers receive extensive training in *Instrumental Enrichment* techniques and adequate materials to fully implement this model of instruction. Counselors, school psychologists, and central office personnel receive training in dynamic assessment, the *Learning Potential Assessment Device* (LPAD), to assist in the diagnosis of learning deficits and the formulation of individual learning plans for students. Special-needs students are given both individualized instruction and mainstream instruction during the regular school day. Combining the Feuerstein method and the team approach provides an ideal learner-centered environment at the middle school level.

Your Ideas

Middle School Sample Schedule I

8:00–8:50 A.M.   *Instrumental Enrichment* (M-W-F)—Reading Resource (T-Th)

	Teacher 1	Teacher 2	Teacher 3	Teacher 4
9:00–10:00 A.M.	Lang. Arts (A)	Lang. Arts (B)	Sci. (C) Sci. (D)	Math (D) Math (C)
10:00–10:15 A.M.	Break			
10:15 A.M.–12:15 P.M.	Lang. Arts (C)	Lang. Arts (D)	Sci. (A) Sci. (B)	Math (B) Math (A)
12:15–1:00 P.M.	Lunch			
1:00–2:00 P.M.	*Social Studies	Social Studies	Social Studies	Social Studies
2:00–3:15 P.M. 3:15–3:30 P.M.	Exploratories/P.E./Health Reflection on day's work			

*Note that each teacher teaches a social studies unit. Students rotate through the four thematic units during the year, but teachers become experts in their theme.

Middle School Sample Schedule II
The Micro-Society

In Lowell, Massachusetts, and Harlem, New York, teachers have restructured middle schools in the micro-society model. In this approach, all students attend basic skills classes in mathematics, social studies, language arts, and science during the morning session. After lunch, the students regroup in the micro-society. The micro-society is a miniature version of a small business community—including a bank, a grocery store, variety stores, a courthouse, and other business establishments the students choose to operate. In the micro-society, students transfer academic skills from the morning classes to the hands-on community in the afternoon. They produce and market goods, use a currency, follow or break laws they have set up to run the micro-society, and conduct court as needed.

9:00–9:40 A.M.	Mathematics
9:40–10:20 A.M.	Language Arts
10:20–11:00 A.M.	Social Studies
11:00–11:40 A.M.	Science
11:40 A.M.–12:20 P.M.	Lunch
12:20–3:30 P.M.	Micro-Society
3:30 P.M.	Dismissal

IRI/Skylight Publishing, Inc.

Secondary school examples of learner-centered scheduling

The learner-centered classroom at the secondary school level differs substantially from the traditional secondary school classroom. The traditional secondary school schedule is broken into six or seven, forty- or fifty-minute periods. Students rotate through these periods in a fashion reminiscent of a revolving door. They come into the building and go directly to a fifteen-minute homeroom. The homeroom's sole purpose is to establish the fact that the student is present. Most use this time as a social event, catching up on what classmates did the night before. At the ringing of a bell, they jostle each other, clanging lockers and getting materials for first period. After entering the first period class, settling into their seats, and allowing the teacher a moment to determine who is present (again), who is on time, who is late, and who brought excuses for yesterday's absences, class begins. They engage in "meaningful tasks" for thirty-five to forty minutes before they begin to gather their things together in anticipation of the next bell. This procedure is carried out at least six times, often more, during the average secondary school day. Most adults would cringe if subjected to the disjointed activities endured daily by secondary students. How can meaningful learning occur when students are literally jumping from subject to subject with no opportunity to make associations and integrate the knowledge into their lives?

Joseph Caroll (1993) describes an alternative to this ritual. He appropriately calls it the Copernican Plan, because his ideas may revolutionize the century-old structure of the high school.

Simply, the Copernican Plan deploys staff and students to allow for more effective teaching. Schedules increase class time for each subject and allow the student to concentrate on only one or two subjects at a time. This improves both instruction and student performance. Macroclasses meet for either 226 minutes for thirty days

*Your
Ideas*

for one subject or 110 minutes for sixty days for two subjects (see proposed schedules).

Fine arts, physical education, seminars, help sessions, and study time are all scheduled in the afternoon. The theory behind this radical schedule change is simple—it allows students to focus on one or two areas, teachers to focus on one or two classes, and gives ample time for in-depth study rather than superficial coverage.

Copernican Plan Sample Schedule I

Time	Schedule A	Schedule B
7:46 A.M.		Macroclass 1 (110 min.) for 60 days
9:36 A.M.	Macroclass (226 min.) for 30 days	
		Passing (6 min.)
9:42 A.M.		Macroclass II (110 min.) for 60 days
11:32 A.M.		
	Passing (6 min.)	
11:38 A.M.		
	First Lunch (35 min.)	Seminar I/Music/Arts (70 min.)
12:13 P.M.		
12:48 P.M.	Seminar II/Music/Arts (70 min.)	
		Second Lunch (35 min.)
1:23 P.M.		
	Passing (6 min.)	
1:29 P.M.		
	Preparation/Help/Study/P.E.	
2:39 P.M.		
	Departure (6 min.)	
2:45 P.M.		
	Activities/Sports (135 min.)	
5:00 P.M.		

IRI/Skylight Publishing, Inc.

Teacher preparation time becomes more efficient, since teachers focus on one or two subjects at a time. Teachers can also give more individual help, because fewer students pass through their classes. An added benefit of the Copernican Plan is the class size reduction. Teachers traditionally teach five classes per day all year long. With this plan, each teacher teaches six classes per year.

The Copernican Plan seems to be an inexpensive alternative to current mailbox secondary school programs. It provides several options with larger blocks of time for instruction. Such creative and effective restructuring can solve some of the problems facing education today.

Another alternative is the School-to-Work Split Schedule. In this model, pioneered by the Boston Public Schools, students in grades 10–12 participate in an occupational internship program. In one version, half of the upper grade students participate in classes, while the second half participates in the intern program at the work site. At midday, the students flip their schedules. In a second version, all upper grade students attend classes in the morning and move to their internship sites in the afternoon.

Your Ideas

School-to-Work Split Schedule

GROUP A		GROUP B	
Period I	Communication	Period I	Work Site
Period II	Mathematics	Period II	Communication
Period III	Science	Period III	Mathematics
Period IV	Work Site	Period IV	Science

Secondary to scheduling concerns in school-to-work internships is the reconceptualization of the curriculum for these students. The school-to-work concept was initiated by teachers who were frustrated with the large number of students who were requesting short-day schedules so they could work in low-paying, dead-end jobs for quick money. The teachers capitalized on the students' preference for money over a high school diploma by searching out internships with local hospitals, social service agencies, and businesses. The student intern jobs provided approximately the same wages as a fast-food job. However, the new classes taught skills directly related to the internship. For instance, students interning in the hospital radiology department were required to take the restructured biology class.

Instead of the general biology curriculum common in most secondary schools, the restructured biology class focused on health care. In addition, the basic biology class became the passkey to advanced classes in anatomy, radiology, and health chemistry. Similarly, students interning in the hospital business department found a new curriculum that gave them business skills. Word processing, spreadsheets, and other analytical tools became immediately useful. These students developed writing skills by learning how to prepare memos and letters to clients, reading skills by studying the procedural manuals, and mathematical skills by using spreadsheets.

The faculty associated with the school-to-work internships extended the curriculum restructuring beyond the classroom work. With the on-the-job personnel, the faculty developed an internship curriculum that would extend class work. Thus, the internship was not just an add-on or an escape from school. It became part of the curriculum monitored daily by the faculty as they accompanied the students to the work site.

A third model for secondary schools involves a two-step restructuring program. Step one divides the school into four houses. Each house has its own core faculty. Students are assigned a house in the first year, but may, for reasons of interest and talent, change houses. After the ninth grade, the curriculum of each house varies. This leads to step two when each house follows a separate curriculum. For instance, house one focuses on technology studies. Its goal is to prepare students for technology careers. Science, mathematics, and language arts classes are studied using technology tools. Other classes, in ninety-minute blocks, allow the students to develop skills in electronic graphics production, technology repair, and software development. In the senior year, students may elect semester-long internships. House two prepares students for college and follows a traditional academic curriculum. Classes are scheduled three days a week for fifty minutes, one day a week for one hundred minutes, and one day is allotted for interdisciplinary topics, special events, and individual projects. House three's curriculum prepares students in the fine and performing arts. Three days per week, the students have a traditional fifty-minute class schedule. Two days per week are allotted for performance practices, special projects, and studio work. House four's curriculum prepares students in general business skills. All upper grade students have a traditional fifty-minute class schedule for three- fourths of the year. Each quarter, one-fourth of the students are off-campus with supervised work-study.

Cooperation

The learner-centered classroom fosters cooperation rather than competition. Tasks are structured to facilitate working collaboratively. Social and cooperative skills are taught as a regular part of the curriculum. Students develop a sense of responsibility to community that easily transfers to real-life situations. The research that indicates that cooperative learning is more beneficial than isolated and competitive learning is put to use by estab-

Your Ideas

lishing base groups, which may function as support teams all year; formal task groups, assigned to complete a project and disassemble; and informal groups formed quickly to discuss or brainstorm ideas.

Mastery of material

Learner-centered classrooms are concerned with mastery rather than coverage of material. Failure is not an option. Students are retaught concepts in different ways until they achieve the skill or objective. Then they progress to the next objective. The alternative school in Bainbridge, Georgia, typifies mastery learning at its best. Students who have failed two or more grade levels are selected for a program of intense study. This helps each student master discrete skills to enable him or her to move more quickly into high school programs. Over 90 percent of these students complete the objectives, continue into high school, and perform at B or above levels, testifying to the effectiveness of mastery programs.

Internal motivation

Learner-centered classrooms stress intrinsic motivation. When students successfully master meaningful tasks, they are encouraged to reach for higher objectives. Success and pride in learning become the rewards. Self-esteem is not taught as a separate subject. Instead the student's competence in completing meaningful work creates the self-confidence that builds self-esteem without artificial curricula designed to make the child "feel good."

Learner responsibility by demonstration

In the learner-centered classroom, students are taught an explicit skill, such as listening without interrupting. After an intense lesson focusing only on that skill, students are expected to demonstrate newly acquired skill in subsequent lessons as other content is introduced. For example, if, on Monday, students are taught the skill of disagreeing politely, in subsequent lessons in social studies, science, and math, students would be expected to practice their skill of "disagreeing politely."

Your Ideas

Staff development/long-term collaboration

Possibly the biggest difference between the learner-centered and the traditional school is staff development. Learner-centered teachers look for new and more effective ways of reaching students. The teachers are given time to talk among themselves. These conversations generate the questions and topics that form the nucleus of staff development. The teachers ask genuine questions and expect well-researched, genuine answers that will improve their instruction. Their interest is real and they are far more likely to implement innovative ideas and keep trying until they are successful.

The staff development committee in Wheaton, Illinois, meets in the spring of each year to poll faculty about anticipated staff development needs. Based on faculty input, workshops, classes, seminars, observations, visits, and other methods, staff developments are planned. During the following year, these plans are carried out. Occasionally, the staff determines a need during the school year. Subcommittees are then formed to research the area in need and make recommendations for further study.

The Scarsdale Teachers Institute in Scarsdale, New York, polls the faculty in small groups several times during the year about anticipated staff development needs. Based on faculty input, workshops, classes, seminars, observations, visits, or other methods, staff developments are planned. During the school year these plans are carried out.

Your Ideas

Flat organization

In the 1960s, Volvo of Sweden shocked the auto-making world by eliminating the assembly line and instituting team-based production. Each team comprises seven to ten car assemblers who work together to build a single car at a time. The team decides among its members who does what, including quality checks.

By 1985, General Motors decided it would produce a new auto, the Saturn, by using the team-assembly approach in a flat organizational structure.

The flat organization flattens or removes the layers of management found in the hierarchical model. The General Motors auto division, except for Saturn, employs the hierarchial method with up to twenty-nine layers of supervisory management between the CEO and the assemblers. Because the Saturn plants produce a better car at a lower price, the other divisions are restructuring to follow the flat organization example.

Learner-centered schools in Massachusetts, Illinois, and Minnesota have flattened their organizational structures. In Massachusetts, the school faculty, divided into teams, makes all decisions about curriculum, instruction, scheduling, and student placement. They also hire a manager who reports to the faculty council. The manager is responsible for maintaining the physical facility, buses, and supplies.

In Chicago, Illinois, the state legislature mandated a decentralization of schools. Each school, led by a local school council of elected teachers, parents, and community members, hires the principal for a four-year contract. The principal carries out the plans of the local council, and controls his or her school's curriculum and instruction. Neither the central office nor the district offices influence principal selection or the operation of the school.

In Minnesota, teachers operate without a principal. An elected operations team oversees the day-to-day func-

IRI/Skylight Publishing, Inc.

tions of the school. Other teacher teams guide the curriculum, instruction, and assessment programs.

Shared leadership

In the flat organization, leadership tends to be shared. In the Volvo and Saturn plants, leadership rotates among team members. In learner-centered schools, multiple leaders appear in different task groups. In the Minnesota school, the steering council consists of members elected from task groups. The chair position rotates annually. In the Massachusetts school, no leadership position is designated. Instead, the school team meets, and each individual takes on specific responsibilities.

When leadership is shared, supervision becomes obsolete. As advocated by Deming, fear engendered by evaluation gives way to collaborative assistance and internal motivation. Peer coaching, team goals, and a shared vision of excellence become the tools for moving the flat organization along the improvement path. Rather than continue the practice of using evaluation by a supervisor as the external motivator of individual performance, the flat organization provides opportunities for the entire team to collaborate in achieving a single organizationwide goal.

Systemic change through Total Quality Leadership

One systemic model for creating the learner-centered school is Deming's Total Quality Leadership. What Deming's Total Quality is to business, learner-centeredness is to education. The challenge of education in the year 2000 and beyond is to create opportunities for our students that promote the intellectual, work, and social skills necessary for tomorrow's citizens. The same systemic standards apply to schools and businesses attempting to implement quality principles. Deming and his Detroit study group identified eight principles for

Your Ideas

*Your
Ideas*

schools desiring Total Quality. The International Renewal Institute is using an innovative grant from the Department of Education to help twenty-two schools in three states employ these principles to institute learner-centeredness:

- Constancy of purpose
- Reduced dependence on testing
- Continuous improvement of the system
- Continuous training and development
- Leadership development
- Elimination of fear as a motivator
- Elimination of work based on quotas
- Empowered stakeholders

It only takes a moment to realize that the eight principles are inherent in the learner-centered school. Placing the learner at the center of the school target provides the constancy of purpose Deming stresses in his principles. The school keeps the students' needs at the center of the target, and the entire school functions around the students' best interests.

Obviously, in such a school, authentic assessment of authentic learning prevails. Standardized testing decreases. Students would engage in real-life, meaningful tasks to demonstrate their mastery of skills. And, in engaging in meaningful tasks, students continuously improve their mastery of skills.

Becoming a Total Quality school requires a basic rethinking of the current educational system. Teachers are not information givers, doling out curriculum to passive learners who memorize facts for tests and promptly forget them. Merely covering material is not acceptable for students. The quality school focuses on:

- Meeting the developmental needs of a changing student population;
- Addressing the at-risk and early childhood populations;

Your Ideas

- Increasing student achievement through self-monitoring performance processes, authentic assessment practices, and continuous quality improvement;
- Maintaining high expectations for all student learners; and
- Encouraging extensive family and parental involvement in the education of their young people.

In addition, the system must

- Be designed to affirm the dignity and worth of all who participate in it;
- Be prepared to deal with students at their individual levels of knowledge, skills, and attitudes when they enter the system;
- Focus on encouraging individuals to assume responsibility for their own behavior and performance;
- Provide opportunities at every level for all who will be involved in carrying out decisions about the quality of learning;
- Provide a climate that encourages innovation and creativity;
- Believe that accountability is an essential ingredient at all levels of the educational system. Accountability must be coupled with sufficient control over the conditions for success and the authority necessary to make decisions and carry them out effectively; and
- Operate well in a site-based model where faculty administrators share decisions.

3

How does a school become learner-centered?

As society changes, schools and systems supporting those schools must change, too. But change is gradual, and the primary reason for failure of new programs is the lack of time provided for teachers, parents, students, and the community to accept and support the change. A successful transition from the factory system to the learner-centered system requires two types of change:

1. Systemic change—change that occurs throughout the entire institution.
2. Individual change—personal change that occurs when the individual believes the change is necessary and beneficial.

Your Ideas

Systemic change comes about only if there is genuine collaboration among parents, the community, and the school. All must agree on the common goal—preparing students to live and work in the twenty-first century. Study groups or committees can be formed to research and discuss the emerging information on learning. With a fundamental understanding of learning, the study groups can move toward an understanding of the connection between curriculum instruction and assessment. They need to see the integration of high standards, learner-centered instruction, and authentic assessment.

As school study groups discover these integrated connections and learn more about the process of change, they can develop a vision for their school as a learning system. This vision becomes the goal, the reason behind all innovations and changes. Next, collaborative teams develop annual action plans that move the school system closer to the vision. This group sets benchmarks that the school will strive to reach during the coming year. At the end of each year, progress can be measured, adjustments made and new benchmarks developed. The process is dynamic and ever-changing. It does not become stagnant or outdated because it is constantly evolving.

Framework for change

Your Ideas

Study groups begin by developing a coherent framework for change. For instance, New York State's *A New Compact for Learning* (1991) establishes the framework for change by encouraging school teams to:

- Develop a coherent vision of learning with outcomes to be sought over the course of each student's schooling;
- Support the development of students' abilities to demonstrate in-depth understanding of core concepts, to think and reason, to use a wide range of communication and information-management skills, and to generate and apply knowledge in real-life situations;
- Foster instruction that nurtures students' imagination, creative vision, and aesthetic appreciation, along with their appreciation for the diversity of human experience and for personal, civic, social, and intellectual values;
- Urge teachers to use a range of teaching strategies that recognize diverse ways of learning and performance and allow for many different kinds of evidence about what students have learned; and
- Encourage schools to teach in interdisciplinary ways and to use other learning settings, including libraries, museums, businesses, and community organizations.

To start the process of change, the study groups must set the learner outcomes expected at the end of the first year. It is important in developing these outcomes that they meet two criteria:

1. They must be meaningful.
2. They must focus on results.

IRI/Skylight Publishing, Inc.

*Your
Ideas*

New York State's *A New Compact for Learning* details these outcomes that focus on results. It encourages performance standards for learning:

- Be as authentic as possible, representing real-world tasks and situations requiring higher-order thinking and complex, integrated performances;
- Provide multiple ways for students to demonstrate their skill, knowledge, and understanding, including written and oral examinations, performance tasks, projects, portfolios, and structured observations by teachers;
- Enable teachers to assess student growth in a cumulative, longitudinal fashion using many kinds of evidence;
- Be measures of actual performance which can be easily expressed, used, and understood by students, parents, teachers, counselors, and the public;
- Communicate expectations and support student motivation, self-assessment, and continual growth;
- Use criteria that are open and clearly articulated so they can guide teaching and learning;
- Inform instruction and encourage reflective practice; and
- Be valid and accurate for identifying students' strengths, abilities, and progress, opening up possibilities for encouraging further growth rather than precluding access to future, advanced instruction.

Such standards lead naturally to schools composed of learner-centered classrooms with these benefits:

1. Individual differences are celebrated and competition reduced.
2. Students can practice interpersonal skills and develop feelings of individual self-worth.

IRI/Skylight Publishing, Inc.

3. The diverse nature of the families from which students come and the larger society to which they will move are honored.

4. It is easier and more acceptable for students to find and work at their own levels because of the wide range of materials and learning experiences available. This leads to a greater sense of pride in achievement.

5. Students benefit from exploring issues from varying points of view.

6. Because the student works with others of different levels of maturity, the sense of community and cooperation is enhanced.

7. Students make stronger connections and see interrelationships among subjects.

8. Students have a more positive attitude toward school and learning.

9. Assimilation into groups seems to be easier for new students.

10. Greater flexibility is available in the placement of students in appropriate settings.

11. Students see themselves as part of a continuum.

12. Opportunities exist for in-depth evaluation by teachers and more self-evaluation.

13. Students are more likely to be both leaders and followers, reinforcing peer evaluation and learning.

14. Students, parents, and teachers are able to form more meaingful relationships.

15. Continuous progress is a more accessible reality.

Your Ideas

*Your
Ideas*

Your School's Scale

To test your school, set up a continuum for each of these fifteen items. Ask the question, "To what degree does . . .

To what degree does your school accept individual differences and reduce or eliminate competition?

```
        3                           2                           0
        |---------------------------|---------------------------|
     Totally                    Somewhat                   Not at all
```

To what degree do you accept individual differences and reduce or eliminate competition?

```
        3                           2                           0
        |---------------------------|---------------------------|
     Totally                    Somewhat                   Not at all
```

Create a questionnaire and tabulate your school's or your classroom's results.

Question:_____


```
        3                           2                           0
        |---------------------------|---------------------------|
     Totally                    Somewhat                   Not at all
```

Question:_____


```
        3                           2                           0
        |---------------------------|---------------------------|
     Totally                    Somewhat                   Not at all
```

Question:_____


```
        3                           2                           0
        |---------------------------|---------------------------|
     Totally                    Somewhat                   Not at all
```

Question:_____


```
        3                           2                           0
        |---------------------------|---------------------------|
     Totally                    Somewhat                   Not at all
```

Time for change

When schools make the fundamental changes required for a systemic shift, school leadership must provide the time needed for thinking, collaborating, planning, and problem solving. Teachers need time to plan as individuals and as a part of the teams working on the schoolwide restructuring effort. Short-term plans should dovetail with the long-range plan for the total educational experience of each student. Since the learner-centered classroom is not textbook bound, it is important to establish expectations for learning throughout the entire program. This ensures that all students receive instruction without gaps and discrepancies in acquired skills. Teachers must continuously adjust their learning environment to meet the needs of each student, a task that requires daily thought, preparation, and time. Scheduling and flexible teaching also require planning time. As they try various new techniques and strategies, teachers need additional time for coaching during staff development sessions. Consequently, collaborative teams should devise creative schedules that allow adequate time for all the activities so essential to a successful transition.

Time for Change

Purchased time. A district pays teachers for coming in during vacations or over the summer, or a fund pays substitutes to take over classes. This is an ideal option for the curriculum development phase. Teachers who meet during their vacations are less tired and more enthusiastic about their task, which shows in the quality of their curriculum design.

Borrowed time. Each school day is lengthened by a few minutes so that students can eventually be released for a partial day of teacher planning. Or, in team teaching, team members alternate between teaching and planning. The lengthened day is a creative approach to finding planning time that most parents understand and support. Unfortunately, many states have number-of-day requirements that need to be waived to allow the lengthened day to succeed.

Common time. The entire day is rescheduled so several teachers will have the same free period. This strategy is very helpful to teachers implementing multiage grouping or interdisciplinary integrated studies.

IRI/Skylight Publishing, Inc.

*Your
Ideas*

Freed-up time. Student teachers, parents, community members, volunteers, or administrators take on teacher tasks or classes. One school used community volunteers for a half day every Wednesday to provide enrichment classes for their K–5 students, while the entire faculty met to design curriculum and plan integrated units.

Better-used time. Faculty meetings deal exclusively with planning, not announcements or administrative details. There should *never* be a meeting when a memo would suffice. Teachers dislike spending time on administrative duties, but are very willing to use their time for collaboration and planning.

New time. Teachers are compensated in new ways—for example, with inservice credit—for using their own time. Often this inservice credit can serve to renew teaching certificates and, in some cases, can be counted as college credit toward advanced degrees.

Rescheduled time. The school calendar is changed to provide more teacher planning days. This may require decreasing students' attendance days or paying teachers for adding days to their contracted year.

(Purnell and Hill, 1992)

What individual change is needed?

Each school comprises individuals. For schoolwide change to occur, these individuals must be willing to undergo personal change in concert with the systemic change developed by the school community.

Hall and Hord (1987) found that change is successful only if attention is given to the concerns of individuals and the specific contexts in which they function. Long-term change occurs only after teachers work through the stages of change and their personal concerns are addressed. They need to understand from the beginning the timelines and expectations, and they need time to progress through the stages of change at their own rates.

Your Ideas

Beginning steps of change

Stage one: What's in it for me?

The first stage for most people is the "what's in it for me?" stage. Initially teachers, students, and parents want to know how the change will impact their lives. It is important at this time that the risk factors be reduced so that those involved in making the change know they will not be penalized for making mistakes. This stage establishes the foundation for lasting change. Dialogue among administrators, teachers, students, parents, and staff developers becomes the focal point for setting the priorities, procedures, and background for the program

Stage two: How do I do this?

After the "what's in it for me?" stage, teachers move into a "how do I do this?" stage. At this point in the change process, it is important to introduce the change to students, parents, and community if they have not already been involved. Gaining the support and understanding of students, parents, and community helps prevent the conflict that newness and uncertainty bring to the classroom. All of the people involved need to know and understand what's in it for them and how the change will be implemented. Teachers, at this point, are very vulnerable. They have risked trying new ideas, and need coaching. Traditionally, the leadership of the school serves to evaluate teacher performance. But in the quality school, leaders must model the type of teaching they want the teachers to use with students, structure collaborative planning time, and encourage application of new methods in the classroom.

As the teacher applies new methods, he or she must tell students, parents, and community about how the new concept will be implemented in the classroom, what is expected of students and parents, and how the change will affect everyone in school. To those who graduated during the past forty years, school may mean straight

IRI/Skylight Publishing, Inc.

rows, notes, long lectures, workbooks, and tests. Any variance needs to be explained in terms of benefits, research findings, and the background of learner-centered education in order to gain support for the program.

Researchers identify that understanding and support by teachers and parents are the most crucial factors in the success of any new program. And if parents are to give their support, teachers must convince them of the merits of the program.

In 1990 and 1991, a survey of ten ungraded primary programs by the Kentucky Education Association and the Appalachia Educational Laboratory (Raymond, 1992) indicated that the leading factor in program failure was lack of teacher and parent understanding and acceptance of the nongraded program concept. Typically, in any new program, attention must be given to ensuring understanding and acceptance by all involved.

Both parents and teachers are more likely to support new programs if they participate in the planning and decision-making phases of the implementation. Their input gives them a sense of ownership, a deeper understanding, and the open communication necessary to foster support for the program.

Stage three: Is it making a difference?

In the third stage, teachers want to know if the new technique is making a difference. If they have worked hard and have seen no improvement in their students, teachers tend to revert to traditional practices and the "what's in it for me?" stage. Their new thought may be "why bother with all this work for the same old results?"

At this crucial stage the leader should provide feedback and encouragement to keep the change process moving forward. This support takes three forms:

1. As teachers, parents, and students go through the change process, they need to be aware that at times they will be uncomfortable. All need time to become

Your Ideas

Your Ideas

comfortable with the new concept. The process of implementation cannot happen overnight. Conversations with teachers in other schools and districts who are also engaged in the study and implementation of learner-centered concepts should become a part of the school's staff development.

2. "What the research says" study groups can assist with refinement of the new methods. If these study groups work as problem solvers, they can examine what is working for them, how it relates to the research, and what adaptations will help. It also prevents "throwing out the baby with the bath water."

3. If the support teams design new lessons together, adapt lessons to personal styles, and watch each other teach, the members can help each other reflect and adapt. Team member journals, student artifacts, and classroom peer observations are valuable tools in lesson planning.

Individual Change in a System

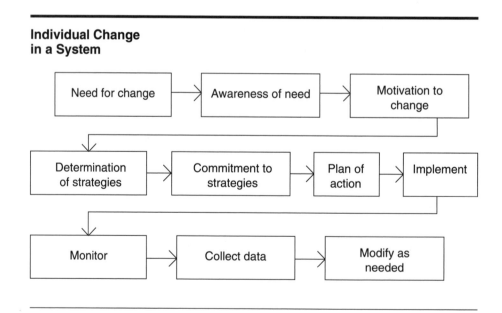

Making a successful transition

Your Ideas

Implementing learner-centered approaches requires a transition from the old to the new. Students, accustomed to straight rows, dittos, lectures, and tests need time to move toward whole language, the writing process, hands-on science and math, cooperative learning, and centers for discovery learning. Parents, too, need a gradual phase-in. During this stage, teachers, students, parents, and the community ask the question, "How can we organize to save time and energy?" The answer is to engage in team-building activities so they develop rapport that enables them to work well together.

As teachers plan toward more learner-centered instruction, resources need to be studied, needs assessed, and allocations made for the coming period of change. At this point, a schoolwide leadership committee should be formed with parent, community, and teacher members. This committee should survey the faculty to determine the instructional requirements that will make the vision a reality. The committee should also prioritize needs and research ways to fund and allocate resources such as equipment, supplies, curriculum, training, space, time, and technology. Committee members also determine what kinds of assessment best fit learner-centered instruction. What procedures for assessment are to be followed? If assessment takes a different form, is it more or less expensive? How are parents trained so that they understand and support the assessment process?

In addition to surveying the logistical needs, a committee establishes procedures and practices that facilitate a close working relationship between school and home. This committee may establish a school volunteer program, a parent training program, and a newsletter or other communication tools that ensure understanding

IRI/Skylight Publishing, Inc.

Your Ideas

and conflict resolution. It sets the tone for parent involvement in the school and ensures that parents are represented on all decision-making teams.

A number of transition tasks are best done by teams. The two most important teams will restructure curriculum and the teacher's role.

The curriculum team addresses curricula, the heart of the school. This team, with input from students, teachers, parents, and community, determines the goals and objectives of the school. This committee also determines and designs thematic units and models of curricular integration that work for the school, the students, and the teachers. They design the instruction of explicit thinking skills and provide the structure for meaningful, relevant problem solving for students. This committee needs the input and support of everyone involved in the change to determine what students need to know and how students learn best.

The teacher role committee studies and defines the teacher's role, because the teacher in a learner-centered classroom has a different role from the traditional teacher. The new role requires the teacher to be less an information giver and more a facilitator of learning and a mediator of cognition. The learner-centered teacher structures tasks as student performances in which each child discovers knowledge. Rather than relying on grades for the primary motivation, the teacher creates meaningful tasks, projects, and other learning experiences that motivate children to want to explore and to learn.

Many other tasks merit teamwork over individual work. After all, many hands make light work. Each school should construct its own teams. In every case, it is important that schoolwide implementation be organized as a coordination of effort, not as another autocratic hierarchy.

Coordination of Effort

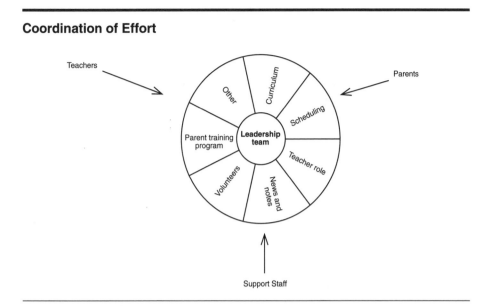

As the various subteams move forward, the leadership team creates and coordinates the new schedule. First the team sets up a timeline for the implementation plan. The table below is an example of a time schedule that might be used in the implementation of any innovative program. The complexity of the program dictates the pace for study, implementation, evaluation, and expansion of the concept. If teachers, parents, and community are undertaking a radical change requiring a great deal of staff training, the timeline for implementation needs to be adjusted for effective staff development.

Sample Time Schedule	Year 1	Year 2	Year 3
	Study groups form	Study groups continue	Study groups examine data collected
	Research		Revise plans
	Site visits		
	Beginning staff development	Continues	Continues/is revised
	Pilot program	Expand to additional teachers/grades	
	Volunteer teachers	Evaluate success	

IRI/Skylight Publishing, Inc.

What does the research say about the learner-centered classroom?

The highly effective learner-centered classroom starts with *heterogeneous* mixes of students in a variety of models. Learner-centered teachers need a wider range of instructional strategies to involve their students in effective exploratory learning. The students in the learner-centered classroom are sub- grouped heterogeneously by ability, interest, motivation, race, ethnic group, and, more and more, by unique challenges. Subgroups are not static. Students may work in base groups or task groups to improve social skills, use graphic organizers, make exhibits, prepare performances or demonstrations, create projects, or conduct experiments. In each case, the student may work with a new mix of students. In the heterogeneous classroom, cooperation is a classroom goal, not a group goal. In addition to the group mixes, the curriculum

itself has a new mix. The curriculum may be thematic,
interdisciplinary, or content-centered. When considering
the research about what works, schools may look in a
variety of places.

Target

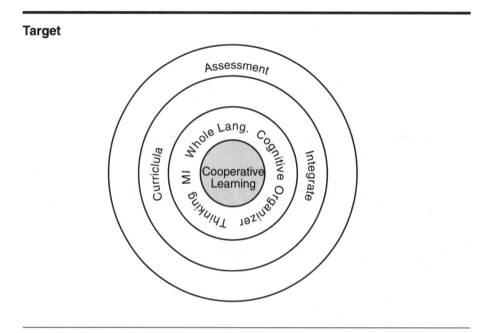

Learner-centered instructional models

Just as the target of the learner-centered school places
the student in the center ring, the target on the research
about most effective learner-centered strategies puts
cooperative learning in the center ring. In their 1988
analysis of the most effective models of teaching (*Student
Achievement Through Staff Development*, ASCD), researchers Joyce and Showers wrote that cooperative
learning is ideal for all curricula, especially the more
complex areas. In *Models of Teaching*, Joyce and Weil
(1986) noted that cooperative learning combined with
higher-order thinking always generated the most powerful

results in achievement, self-concept, and student responsibility than other models they researched.

No contradiction exists between the group thrust and the individual thrust in the learner-centered classroom. The group effort, as the Johnsons have demonstrated, contributes to the greater achievement of each individual in the group. When one person takes over and is the only one to benefit, there is no cooperative learning. There is only selfish, me-focused learning by one and abnegation of learning by the others in the group. A cooperative group by definition is a heterogeneous group that works together to achieve a common goal.

The major findings

The research indicates clearly why cooperative learning is such a critical instructional tool, *essential* to successful learning in the heterogeneous classroom.

- Students who learn in the cooperative model perform better academically than students who learn in the individualistic or competitive models. In their meta-analysis of 122 studies, Johnson and Johnson et al. (1981) showed that cooperative learning tended to give higher achievement results than the other two methods, especially with such higher-level tasks as problem solving, concept attainment, and predicting.

- Because of the quality of "cognitive rehearsal," all students of all ability levels in cooperative learning groups enhance their short- and long-term memory as well as their critical thinking skills (Johnson and Johnson, 1983).

- Because cooperative experiences promote positive self-acceptance, students improve their learning, self-esteem, enjoyment of school, and motivation to participate (Johnson and Johnson, 1983).

- Because cooperative learning leads to positive interaction among students, intrinsic learning motivation

*Your
Ideas*

and emotional involvement in learning are highly developed (Johnson and Johnson, 1989).

• Because cooperative learning nurtures positive peer relationships and structures positive interactions, students in cooperative learning classrooms develop stronger scholastic aspirations, more pro-social behavior, and more positive peer relationships (Johnson and Johnson, 1979; Johnson and Matross, 1977).

Cooperative learning encompasses a variety of successful approaches. Although researchers agree that cooperative classrooms produce superior academic, social, and personal results, they debate which is the "best" approach. Because few practitioners can isolate classroom practice to obtain the "purity" desired by the researchers, most classroom teachers adopt a single approach or a combination of cooperative approaches that work best with their own teaching styles and their own students. Ironically, the research on staff development tells us that the most effective practitioners are more likely to pull the best from each cooperative learning approach and create their own applications.

Model 1: The conceptual approach

Roger Johnson, a science educator, and his brother, David Johnson, a social psychology researcher, use their early studies of cooperative learning to frame the conceptual approach. They argue that all effective cooperative learning includes five critical characteristics. If all five are present, there is cooperative learning. If any one is missing, there may be group work, but not cooperative learning (Johnson, Johnson, and Holubec, 1988).

Your Ideas

The Five Elements of Cooperative Groups

1. **Face-to-face interaction.** The physical arrangement of students in small, heterogeneous groups encourages them to help, share, and support each other's learning.
2. **Individual accountability.** Each student is responsible for the success and collaboration of the group and for mastering the assigned task.
3. **Cooperative social skills.** Students are taught, coached, and monitored in the use of cooperative social skills, which enhance the group work.
4. **Positive interdependence.** Students are structured by a common goal, group rewards, role assignments, and other means to assist each other in completing the learning task.
5. **Group processing.** Students reflect on how well they work as a group to complete the task and how they can improve their teamwork.

In any cooperative lesson, these characteristics overlap. The characteristics are identified to reinforce the notion that all groups are not necessarily cooperative groups. As mental "coat hooks," the characteristics provide a framework for designing strong and effective cooperative learning tasks. They also provide an umbrella under which a large variety of cooperative strategies, structures, and activities may be gathered. As the teacher designs a cooperative lesson, these characteristics are the check list to ensure the greatest success.

Model 2: The curriculum approach

Slavin's research, conducted with colleagues at the Johns Hopkins University Center for Research on Elementary and Middle Schools, focuses on cooperative learning and basic skill instruction. Slavin and his colleagues have developed cooperative curriculum programs in math and language arts. They have prescribed specific cooperative strategies that teachers can easily integrate as they promote heterogeneous cooperation. Because they desire to find workable alternatives to tracking and ability-grouping practices, especially where those practices are detrimental to poor and minority children, they stress packages that all teachers can easily use.

Your Ideas

Slavin's Curriculum Packages

1. Team Accelerated Instruction (TAI)
2. Cooperative Integrated Reading and Composition (CIRC)
3. Teams, Games, Tournaments (TGT)
4. Student Teams, Achievement Division (STAD)

1. **Team Accelerated Instruction (TAI)** is a mathematics program combining cooperative learning with individualized instruction in a heterogeneous classroom. Designed for grades three to six, TAI uses students tutoring each other to encourage accurate work, to produce positive social effects, and to handle the record-keeping logistics of individualized instruction or programmed learning. Every eight weeks, teams of high, middle, and low achievers take achievement tests for placement in the individualized program. In the teams, students help each other through the material. Each day, the teacher pulls students from the heterogeneous groups for focused instruction. Students work in and across teams to progress through the material. Each week, progress scores are established for each team. Criteria are established for the degrees of recognition each team receives.

   TAI dispells the myth that math instruction *must* be done by tracking or ability grouping. TAI students of all abilities do better at computation in concepts and at applications, and improve in self-concept, enjoyment of math, behavior, relations, and acceptance of differences (Slavin, 1984).

2. **Cooperative Integrated Reading and Composition (CIRC).** Slavin's cooperative curriculum for language arts, grades three and four, uses cooperative methods for reading groups (eight to fifteen

students) and reading teams (two or three students). As students work in their teams, they earn points for their groups. Points earned on quizzes, essays, and book reports allow students to earn certifications. Teams can use a variety of strategies while the teacher monitors progress or instructs other teams in comprehension strategies (e.g., predicting, comparing, drawing conclusions). Included in the strategies are partner reading, story prediction, words-aloud practice, spelling review, partner checking, and team comprehension games. At times, students work individually doing independent reading, basal work, or book reports.

CIRC research results demonstrate the benefits of cooperative learning with mainstreamed handicapped students without detriment to the highest-performing students. In the studies, high, medium, and low performers showed equal gains, although the mainstreamed handicapped gains were most impressive (Slavin et al., 1989).

3. **Teams, Games, Tournaments (TGT),** maybe the most widely known of the Slavin/Johns Hopkins curricular approaches, is adaptable to any curricular area, K–12. In this format, students work in groups to master content provided by the teacher. After practicing on worksheets, students demonstrate mastery of the content in weekly tournaments. Students compete in teams against other teams of equal ability (e.g., top achievers vs. top achievers) (Slavin, 1986).

4. **Student Teams, Achievement Division (STAD).** STAD was designed by Slavin and the Johns Hopkins Group in 1982 (Slavin, 1986). In these heterogeneous groups, four or five students of mixed ability, ethnicity,

Your Ideas

Your Ideas

and gender work on work sheets that have the answers provided. The common goal is to understand the answers, not fill in the blanks. The teams quiz each other until all members understand the answers. Then the teacher individually quizzes each member. The team score is the sum of the improvement points earned by each individual. Special recognition is given to the teams with the greatest improvement.

Model 3: The structural approach

Since 1967, Spencer Kagan has researched the structural approach to cooperative learning. This approach incorporates the creation, analysis, and application of *content-free* structures that cause students to interact in positive ways. Content-free structures, usable with any content, enable the teacher to make multiple applications of a single structure in a variety of subjects. (The debate about content-free structures and content-specific structures ensues, it seems, whenever skill-theorists get together. Their debates on study skills, thinking skills, social skills, and reading skills have similar dialogues. Research shows that both content-free and content-specific structures produce positive effects, but there is little proof one method is superior to the other.)

Kagan's structures fall into three groups:

Kagan's Structures

A. **In turn.** The teacher structures a task in which individuals take a turn in a prescribed order. Included among these are "round robin" or "response in turn," "round table," "four corners," and "three-step interview."

B. **Jigsaw.** The teacher structures the task so that each student in the group has part of the information to study. When all members teach each other their material, the whole is greater than the parts. "Level I jigsaw," "level II jigsaw," "co-op—co-op," and "think-pair-share" all follow this format.

C. **Match-ups.** The teacher structures student-to-student tasks, which formally and informally create cooperative situations. Included here are "match mind," "numbered heads together," "co-op cards," and "partners."

Model 4: The constructivist model

Research by Vygotsky (1986), Feuerstein (1980), Sternberg (1986), and Gardner (1983) laid the psychological foundation for the constructivist notion of learning. Their notion is at the heart of a new view of learning for all. Bellanca and Fogarty (1991), started with a constructivist philosophy, and molded the cognitive-cooperative model. This model synthesizes constructivist theories with the best practices of cooperative learning from many models. This gives the classroom teacher a powerful tool for accelerating learning. Rather than having the teacher mediate individual learning with every child, this cooperative model helps the students help each other "make sense" of what they are learning. Many tools and strategies found in the other models are used, but *for a different purpose.* Cognitive-cooperative learning fits the ideal of Joyce and Showers' (1988) study combining methods that promote higher-order thinking rather than having students work in cooperation to complete workbooks, do math computation, or other lower-order tasks found in the traditional factory system.

James Bellanca, Robin Fogarty, and Elizabeth Cohen have built their approaches to cooperative learning on the constructivist model. Cohen's (1986) cooperative approach features "complex learning tasks" for young children. Bellanca and Fogarty (1991), Bellanca (1992), Fogarty (1991), and Fogarty and Bellanca (1987) use the BUILD model (see page 70) to facilitate the synthesis of thinking and cooperating as tools for learning.

In the constructivist model, the research is applied by combining cooperative learning with complex cognition. The mind-brain research provides many ways for teachers to approach cognition and promote student thinking in a cooperative framework.

The constructivist model of cooperative learning uses the BUILD acronym to illustrate the components which purposefully emphasize higher-order thinking in every classroom learning task.

Your Ideas

The Elements of BUILD

B = Build in higher-order thinking so students are challenged to think deeply and to transfer subject matter.

U = Unite the class so students form bonds of trust, which enable teamwork.

I = Individual learning: Each student is accountable to master all skills and knowledge. The groups are a means to facilitate mastery before the teacher checks each individual through quizzes, tests, essays, or other more authentic assessment strategies.

L = Look back and debrief *what* and *how* students learned. Students are taught to "process" or "evaluate" their thinking, feelings, and social skills. This emphasis on "taught" student evaluation shifts the responsibility for learning from the teacher to student.

D = Develop students' social skills. By providing explicit training in the social skills, the teacher helps students master cooperative abilities during cooperative work.

Bellanca & Fogarty (1991, p. 2)

Critical and creative thinking across the curriculum

In the past decade, educators have begun to recognize that critical and creative thinking is not merely an add-on to basic curriculum, but is an essential ingredient in any curriculum that intends to prepare students for the twenty-first century. But many ask, what is the best way to help students develop this ability? Research has attempted to answer that question. Following are three of the most crucial findings.

1. It does no good to teach critical and creative thinking as isolated activities (Fogarty et al., 1992).
2. All children can and must develop their capabilities as critical and creative thinkers (Feuerstein et al., 1980).
3. It is necessary to teach children how to transfer critical and creative thinking across the curriculum (Perkins and Salomon, 1988).

Translating these findings into classroom practice has taken several different and successful approaches. Included in the most successful approaches are the explicit skills approach, the strategic learning approach, the use of cognitive organizers, and the introduction of metacognitive learning.

Your Ideas

Explicit skills approach

This approach identifies the critical and creative thinking skills already implicit in the curriculum and reformats them for explicit instruction. For example, in most fourth grade reading programs, inferring is an emerging skill. Inferring is immersed in the types of activities that students are asked to do as they read. The teacher, informed by the teacher's guide, is expected to encourage students to draw inferences. Better students are expected to begin developing the skill at this point and the others are expected to gradually "get it" in the latter years.

Rather than keep the skill in inferring a teachers' secret and hope that some students will "get it," the explicit skills approach takes a different tack. The teacher identifies the skill to all the children, models how it is done, provides strategies for making inferences, structures practices that focus all students on this critical thinking skill within the day-to-day reading assignments, and mediates their progress in making stronger inferences. At regular instances in other subjects, the teacher encourages students to use the inference strategies they have learned and guides the transfer of inference strategies across the curricular areas.

In addition to inferring, a multitude of other thinking skills are buried in curriculum including predicting (language arts, science, math, social studies), comparing and contrasting (biology, history, social studies), and drawing conclusions (physics, math, language arts). The learner-centered school lends itself well to this approach.

Your Ideas

The explicit skills approach is less concerned with covering a curriculum and more interested in "post holing" key concepts. Therefore, the school team should identify three critical thinking skills to introduce in the year. While the introductory demonstration lessons may take less than sixty minutes, the team does need more time to mediate student use of the skills and to help them make needed transfer across the curriculum. The flexibility built into the daily schedule in the learner-centered school allows the teacher to structure time for the small group and large class discussions that enable students to think through their individual applications.

Strategic learning approach

The strategic learning approach provides tried-and-true, teacher-tested techniques that are ready for immediate use. The strategic learning approach gives the teacher a menu of specific and fully delineated methods for explicit instructional use.

Usually, these strategies are introduced in what is often called a "content-free" lesson. This content-free lesson does indeed have a content focus; however, the content is usually familiar, almost generic in nature. The content merely serves as a vehicle to carry the strategy or skill under study. For example, in teaching the explicit thinking skill of classification, the familiar content focus might be on solids, liquids, and gases. Using these generic categories, the classification skill, not the science, becomes the focus of the lesson.

Similarly, in teaching the strategy PMI (plus, minus, interesting), de Bono (1983) uses the generic or familiar content of buses. The initial lesson requires students to generate pluses, minuses, and interesting aspects of buses that have *no* seats. Again, by using content that is simple and well known, the emphasis falls on the PMI strategy.

The strategic learning approach usually immediately appeals to practitioners because it easily applies directly to the classroom. But the strategies lessons should not be merely taken per se into the classroom as an amusing Friday afternoon activity. When a strategy or skill is used only once, it is an *activity*. If, however, teachers introduce the strategy or skill as modeled, practice it in another situation, and transfer it into still another situation, then and only then can we call it a *strategy*. An activity is a one-time shot. A strategy is used again; it is placed in our repertoire of instructional techniques, our bag of teaching tricks, to be used over and over, whenever appropriate.

Cognitive organizers

The concept of cognitive organizers is rooted in Ausubel's (1978) theory of "meaningful reception learning." Simply put, Ausubel believes that information is stored hierarchically in the brain. For instance, highly generalized concepts seem to cluster together, followed by less-inclusive concepts, and finally specific facts and details.

Cognitive organizers, as studied by Ambruster and Anderson (1980), Dansereau (1979), and Davidson (1982), successfully promote information retention. McTighe and Lyman (1988) demonstrate the use of cognitive organizers in a discussion of "theory-embedded tools" for cognitive instruction. They suggest that the ability to organize ideas is fundamental to thinking. Graphic displays or cognitive maps develop organizational skills for students of all ages and abilities and across all content.

Cognitive organizers provide a holistic picture of the concept, complete with relationships and interrelationships. McTighe and Lyman (1992, p. 81) suggest that cognitive maps help students:

- represent abstract or implicit information in a more concrete form;
- depict relationships between facts and concepts;
- generate and organize ideas for writing;
- relate new information to prior knowledge;
- store and retrieve information; and
- assess student thinking and learning.

*Your
Ideas*

Metacognition–A superordinate kind of thinking

According to Swartz and Perkins (1989), metacognition refers to knowledge about, awareness of, and control over one's own mind and thinking. Costa (1985) calls this "thinking about thinking." Marzano and Arredondo (1986) also speak of awareness and control over one's own thinking, while Brown and Palincsar (1982) describe the metacognitive process in relationship to the reading process.

Brown and Palincsar use the example of the good reader who reads and reads and reads and suddenly hears a little internal voice saying, "I don't know what I just read." The words on the page have been read and spoken in the mind, but in a "word-calling" sense; no meaning has been conveyed. Suddenly, the reader becomes aware of this deficit and his or her mind then signals him or her to adopt a recovery strategy: Reread the beginning of the paragraph, recall a thought, or scan the text for key words.

On the other hand, poor readers read and read and read, never realizing that they aren't comprehending what they have read. They have not noticed that they are not getting meaning from the text, because they have never gotten meaning from text. They "word-call" mentally, but are nonreaders in the real sense of reading.

Like good readers, we must learn to understand and articulate our own mental processes. This necessary link to fruitful transfer or—as Costa (1991) suggests about metacognition—knowing what we know and what we don't know, and wondering why we are doing what we are doing. That's the metacognition we want to promote for all learners.

Planning, monitoring, and evaluating the learning activity are the components of metacognitive processing. Students become aware of their own thinking and what goes on inside their heads when they are thinking prior to, during, and after a learning activity.

IRI/Skylight Publishing, Inc.

Your Ideas

Metacognition

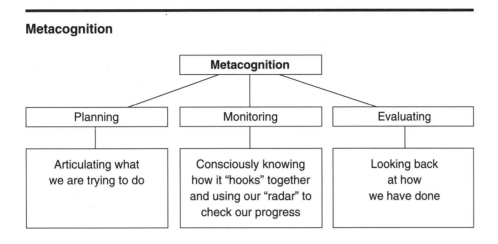

In addition to these cognitive approaches, cooperative learning enriches project-based and problem-based learning. Project-based learning—applying knowledge to make a product, demonstrate a "how-to" process, create an exhibit, or perform—inherently challenges students to do complex thinking. Problem-based learning—identifying and solving a problem using an orderly thought process— also structures students into higher-level thought. Complex tasks are further enhanced when they include thinking tools such as graphic organizers or require students to metacognitively reflect after the task.

Learner-centered classroom research

Research not only heralds the achievement and motivation that springs from cooperative and cognitive instructional strategies, but also points to the value of learner-centeredness in the classroom. For the primary grades, Barbara Pavan summarized the research on the multiage classroom which is one way to create a learner-centered classroom.

Your Ideas

Research on nongraded programs:

1. Research studies comparing nongraded and graded schools provide a consistent pattern favoring nongradedness.

2. The nongraded groups performed better (58 percent) or as well as (33 percent) the graded groups on measures of academic achievement.

3. On mental health and school attitudes, 52 percent of the studies indicated nongraded schools as better for students, 43 percent similar. Only 5 percent showed nongraded as worse than graded schools.

4. The benefits of students of nongradedness increase as students have longer nongraded experiences.

5. Blacks, boys, low socioeconomic level students, and underachievers benefit from a nongraded program.

Pavan (1993, p. 66)

Primary Research

Other learner-centered practices being researched at the primary and elementary level include:

1. **Integration of Gardner's Multiple Intelligences into the content instruction in classrooms.** Gardner's research along with the research on schools using these approaches demonstrates multiple intelligences strategies to be valuable in the learner-centered school (Gardner, 1983). (Chapter 6 explains the multiple intelligences more fully.)

2. **Thematic lessons and units.** Research demonstrates the importance of teaching in interconnected, thematic units of study. Thematic lessons help students make sense of learning by connecting school subjects to real-life situations (Jacobs, 1989). (Thematic planning will be covered in depth in Chapter 6.)

3. **Developmentally appropriate practices.** Developmentally appropriate practices developed along with the multiage, whole language movements in education. Researchers have found that previous expectations about certain behaviors are physically and mentally inappropriate for students in lower grade levels. The learner-centered school takes this research into account and provides activities appropriate to the child's abilities (Fogarty, 1993).

IRI/Skylight Publishing, Inc.

Research emphasizes that the learner and his needs should be at the center of the learning target. Numerous other research studies are being conducted and are shaping what the learner-centered class may become (Pavan, 1993).

Middle School Research

Current research on the middle school also demonstrates the need for the learner-centered classroom. Flexible scheduling, team teaching, interdisciplinary units, and other learner-centered concepts indicate that middle schools are becoming more "student friendly" and less of the old junior high or mini high school prototype.

Secondary Research

Research on the learner-centered secondary school is not as comprehensive as the research on multiage schools for primary students. The research that does exist can be divided into three areas.

1. Cooperative-cognitive strategies are effective instructional tools. The meta-analysis done by Bruce Joyce and Beverly Showers (1988) on effective teaching strategies included studies with secondary students.

2. The research on tracking and ability grouping by Jeannie Oakes, Robert Slavin, and Jomills Braddock II has clearly shown the negative effects of these practices on secondary students, especially poor or minority students.

    "Why, in the light of all the research evidence that tracking is harmful to students in the lower tracks and that high achievers can function well in heterogeneous groups, is the practice so widespread and entrenched in our schools?" (Oakes and Lipton, 1990, p. 187)

    There are several conclusions that can be advanced with some confidence. These are as follows:

    • Comprehensive between-class ability grouping plans have little or no effect on the achievement

Your Ideas

of secondary students. This conclusion is most strongly supported in grades 7–9, but the more limited evidence that does exist from studies in grades 10–12 also fails to support any effect of ability grouping.

• Different forms of ability grouping are equally ineffective.

• Ability grouping is equally ineffective in all subjects, except that there may be a negative effect of ability grouping in social studies.

• Assigning students to different levels of the same course has no consistent positive or negative effects on students of high, average, or low ability" (Slavin, 1993, p. 109).

"Findings on the maldistributions of groups of race/ethnic students in curriculum tracks and ability groups, and the effects of placement in those tracks and groups, have many policy implications for equity and excellence in the American educational system.

"First, . . . clear findings on the effects of curriculum tracking and ability grouping indicate the need for change. There may have been a time when curriculum tracking in schools did actually coincide with the needs of the society and the economy outside of schools—that is, a number of academically proficient students were needed to pursue further education and careers that depended upon that education, while a number of non-academically oriented students were needed to enter the workforce directly and perform the important and even well-paying jobs that required less education. This situation has changed dramatically, but curriculum tracking still exists" (Braddock II, 1993, p. 140).

3. Research that favors heterogeneous classrooms is emerging. Case studies of middle schools and secondary schools that are moving from tracked classes into more heterogeneously mixed classrooms indicate that

not only poor and low-performing students, but gifted and high-performing students benefit.

"Values, history, and politics that include, but go far beyond, matters of pedagogy and human learning underlie school tracking practices. Changing such practices will require the careful, open, tolerant, and generous probing of the experiences, assumptions, values, and knowledge of those whose lives are most affected by it: students, teachers, administrators, and communities. Inquiry, reflection, and thoughtful dialogue among policy makers, practitioners, and their constituents is an arduous and rarely attempted undertaking in education. But we should expect to do no less if we intend to make schools humane, equitable, and truly educational places" (Oakes, 1993, p. 68).

"More research is needed. There is still much to learn about what works in heterogeneous classes and how middle schools can most effectively encourage and challenge a wide range of learners. Meanwhile, the sense of renewal and energy in schools that are in the process of untracking continues to build the momentum for change. As one student sums it up, 'It's a lot more fun to learn. I imagine it's a lot more fun to teach'" (Steinberg and Wheelock, 1993, p. 218–219).

There are several reasons why less research exists on the learner-centered approach in secondary schools. First, the secondary school is more entrenched in the factory system of education than is the primary school. This is especially true in large urban areas where the system is designed to handle large numbers of students. Structure, practices, curriculum, and Carnegie Units make it very difficult to change the way the average secondary school works.

Second, the secondary school seeks to prepare as many students as possible for university entrance. Students pass through a standardized system in preparation

Your Ideas

for the next level of education. Parents whose children do well in this system know that the system is a ticket to college. These parents do not want the system to change. Detracking has the potential of changing the definition of success. Such a change threatens those whose children have succeeded in the traditional system.

Third, teachers have been prepared to teach within the confines of specific specialty areas: American literature, world history, biology, general business, and so on. Their job is to deliver specific content as rapidly as possible. Changing curriculum and instruction from content coverage to learner-centeredness is a large and difficult task, especially when teachers are asked to make the change "on their own time."

The Copernican Plan offers a promising learner-centered approach in secondary schools. It balances the teachers' desire for purity of discipline and the students' needs for one-on-one instruction, closer and friendlier relationships with teachers, and more indepth instruction to improve understanding and retention of content.

Other learner-centered methods for secondary schools have gotten a slow start. Teachers at the secondary school level have seemingly failed to see the "What's in it for me" phase of individual change and have been reluctant to implement many of the ideas being put forward by the experts.

For all grades, at least another decade of research is needed to support the universal applicability of the learner-centered school. The research indicates what is wrong with traditional practices and suggests what is right about the new approaches. But more research is needed on what actually works with students in different communities before there is a conclusive answer.

IRI/Skylight Publishing, Inc.

6

What are the most effective instructional strategies?

After the school resolves scheduling and other programmatic issues to become learner-centered, the next challenge is determining what actually happens in the classroom. The question of which instructional strategies work best is complex. If we return to the two basic questions of education—"What do children need to know?" and "How do they learn best?"—both the instructional goals and the activities designed to reach those goals, become clearer. Some learner-centered strategies work well in the majority of cases. Others are more limited in scope.

IRI/Skylight Publishing, Inc.

Brain-compatible learning strategies

According to Hart (1975), brain-compatible learning is an umbrella term covering a host of theories about how we learn and how we teach. The brain research of the 1960s, 1970s, and 1980s has led cognitive scientists to a new and better understanding of human learning. Unfortunately, very few colleges teach future teachers these concepts, which might enable them to better reach their students.

Hart goes on to explain, early findings in brain research supported the idea that the brain is divided into left and right hemispheres—each responsible for certain aspects of learning and memory. Scientists also discovered that in most humans the right side of the brain is holistic, visual/spatial, and more random, whereas the left functions more sequentially in symbolic fashion. Some subjects seemed to respond better to visual/spatial teaching, stories, and inductive processes, while others liked abstract, written, sequentially presented information. For a time scientists believed that people use one side of their brains predominantly; so subjects were labeled "left- or right-brained." In fact, it has been discovered that people use both sides, the right to conceptualize visually and the left to form the abstract of that visualization. For example, a person hearing the word *dog* may have an image of a dog in mind which is quickly converted to the abstract letters D-O-G if the person is asked to write the word. The hemispheres of the brain are connected through small passages called dendrites, through which electrical impulses flow from side to side. In reality, through communication from side to side, we are more accurately *whole-brained*.

The brain functions as a pattern-seeking device. When a young child sees a dog; hears the word *dog*, and eventually sees the letters D-O-G, that child begins to recognize a pattern—a connection between seeing the image, hearing the word for that image, and, at a more mature age, seeing the abstract symbols that stand for dog as a meaningful pattern.

Teachers who understand these two principles of cognition know they need to provide a number of activities to teach one concept so the students can begin to see the pattern for themselves. Furthermore, teachers must provide experiences that build on the students' prior knowledge. They can then connect the old to the new, see a pattern, and transfer the learning to new situations. Explicit teaching of the thinking and transfer skills must take place for each new learning situation. Teachers cannot assume that learning will transfer to new situations automatically. As any English teacher will attest, teaching punctuation in English class does not ensure that students will use proper punctuation in their science papers. Transfer seldom occurs without explicit teaching for transfer (Fogarty, Perkins, and Barell, 1992).

The following sample lessons use techniques that enable students to have "being there" experiences, give opportunities to discover patterns, and use both right- and left-brained processing. These lessons demonstrate activities teachers have successfully used to facilitate exploratory learning (Hart, 1975).

Your Ideas

The Target for Effectiveness

PRIMARY SCHOOL

What Is It?

Materials: The teacher assembles different small objects (peanuts, beads, dried peas, rice, salt, etc.) in small containers (35 mm film containers are excellent), which are labeled 1, 2, 3, 4, 5, etc.

Task: The students in learning centers or as a group identify the contents by shaking or in any other way except by looking. Students then describe the differences in sounds (pitch, tone, etc.). The teacher repeats the activity by assembling the objects in bags and having students identify by touch. This is repeated for each sense. Students can use a matrix organizer to note differences and find patterns.

		Touch	Smell	Taste	Sight	Sound
1	peanuts					
2	beads					
3	dried peas					
4	rice					
5	salt					

Reflection: After each "experiment," the students tell the teacher "what" was sensed. After the matrix is filled, the students note similarities and differences, tracing patterns among the similarities. The teacher cues but does not answer for the students. After the discussion, several students summarize the ideas.

MIDDLE SCHOOL

Agree/Disagree

Materials: Resource materials on the judicial system, the legal process, and other supporting research materials.

Task: If time and finances permit, students should be taken on a field trip to a courtroom where they witness a trial. After the "being there" experience, students should decide on an issue of relevance to them and appoint plaintiffs, defendants, court reporters, recorders, etc. Each student researches his or her part in the trial and prepares to role-play appropriately. On a predetermined day, students role-play the trial for fellow students, parents, or teachers. A verdict is determined by the judge or the jury, as warranted by the case.

Reflection: Students decide if they agree with the decision of the jury and tell why or why not.

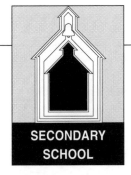

SECONDARY SCHOOL

Molecular Encounters

Materials: The teacher prepares a descriptive story about an atom's journey into several substances, such as water, salt, or air.

Task: Students are asked before beginning a unit on molecular bonding to imagine themselves as atoms. The teacher may then take them on an imaginary trip into the molecules of air, water, salt, etc. After the trip, the teacher might have the students draw or describe what they saw, felt, and heard on the trip. Then the students might be asked to draw the molecules they encountered.

Reflection: The students describe one thing that surprised them about their molecular encounters.

Graphic organizers

An easy way to incorporate whole-brain learning into the classroom is using graphic organizers. These thinking "tools" can effectively enhance students' knowledge and internalization of information. For the child who has high logical/mathematical or visual/spatial intelligence, these organizers bring information and learning to life. Visual images are much easier for these students to remember than abstract words. Teachers probably know some traditional graphic organizers, but often do not use them to their fullest potential in classrooms. Teachers may use a "web" or concept map to organize their thinking about lessons or units of study, but fail to incorporate these tools into the child's learning experience. A student might find it useful to create a web of all the characters from a book or story, such as *Charlotte's Web*.

Literature

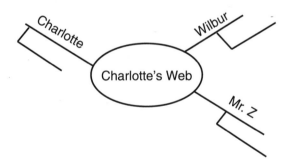

The student can use the diagram to list some interesting details about the character. The same tool might be used to organize attributes in any subject area, as shown in the examples on the next page.

Your Ideas

Math

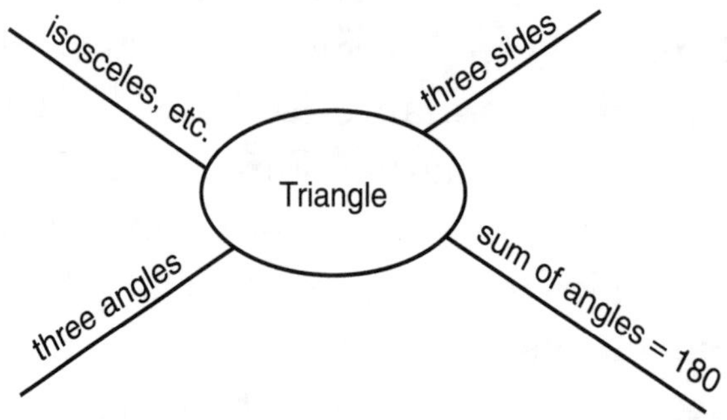

isosceles, etc.   three sides

Triangle

three angles   sum of angles = 180

English

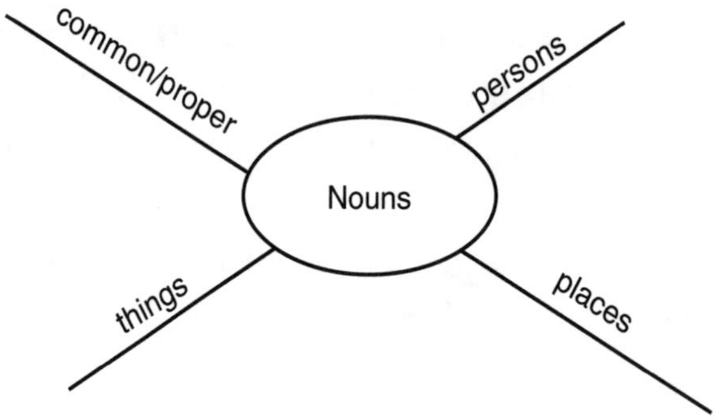

common/proper   persons

Nouns

things   places

Science

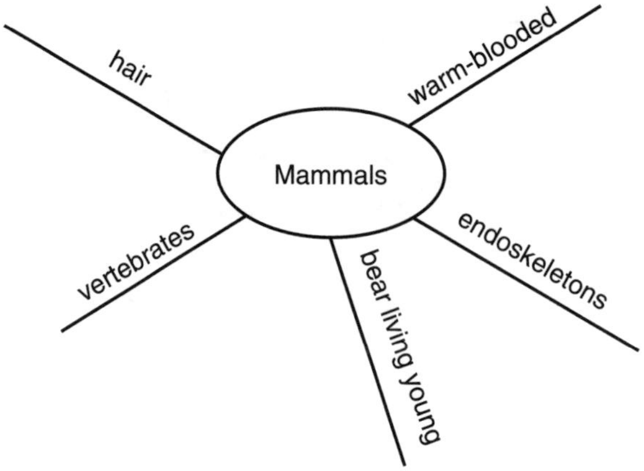

hair   warm-blooded

Mammals

vertebrates   bear living young   endoskeletons

Social Studies

Sherman   Lincoln as president

Civil War characters

Grant   Lee

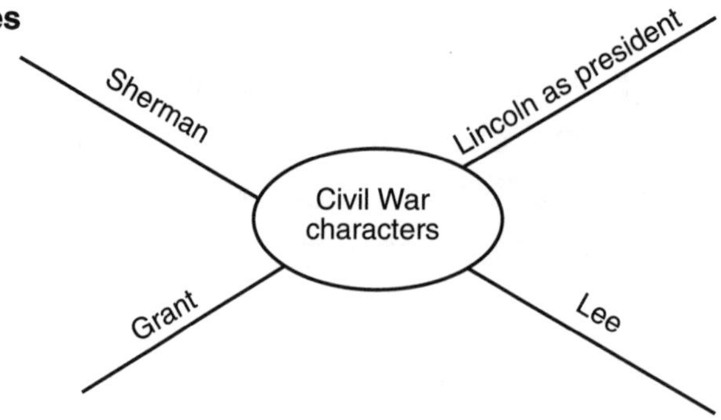

Students often become creative in their web designs, using different shapes to depict the main topic. For example, the topic *Charlotte's Web* could be represented by a spider instead of the center circle. For the triangle web, a triangle might be used.

Students often find the concept map helpful when organizing information for reports or projects. Starting with the concept of a paper or project, the student may use different colored pens to record his or her thoughts about a subject. A student doing a report on a state might use the map to organize the paper.

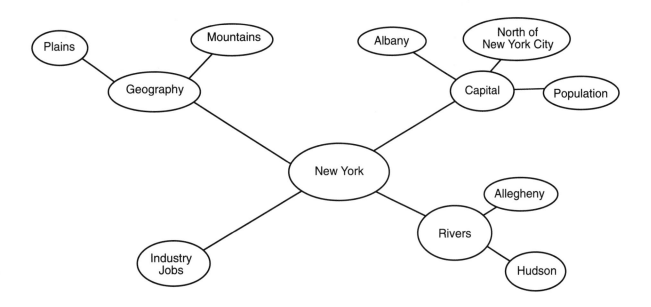

Concepts begin to relate to each other as a student makes an even more detailed inquiry.

*Your
Ideas*

A *matrix* may help students better understand concepts in language arts or science. Biology teacher Bob Kapheim from York High School (Illinois) uses a matrix to study insects. He begins by having students fill in the boxes with the variables for body symmetry, segmentation, form of locomotion, sensory organs, support structures, and body covering. Students then circle randomly a variable in each column to "create a creature." Bob ensures his students' knowledge by having them apply what they know rather than simply remembering. A similar matrix (Bellanca and Fogarty, 1991) has students brainstorm different elements of a story. For example, students are asked to generate a list of heroes, heroines, settings, conflicts, resolutions, and endings for the blank boxes. Having done this, students are given random numbers of boxes to circle. They then create their own short stories using the circled elements.

Matrix

Hero	Heroine	Villian	Setting	Conflict	Resolution	Ending
Batman	Joan of Arc	Joker	New York	Divorce	They won	Lived happily ever after
Superman	Bonnie	Clyde	Wash., D.C.	War	Got killed	Rode into the sunset
J. Edgar Hoover	Cat Woman	Lex Luther	A park	Robbery	Married	Sang "Goodnight, Sweetheart"
Piaget	Florence Nightingale	Snydly Whiplash	By the sea	Fight	Danced the night away	Ascended to the clouds

Using a matrix, teachers can have students create a culture or nation, write a meal menu, design a space station or future car, make a word problem, or analyze pollution samples.

IRI/Skylight Publishing, Inc.

Matrix

Create a sentence:

Nouns	Verbs	Adjectives	Adverbs	Participles	Other

Your Ideas

Using random selection, students can use the above matrix to demonstrate knowledge of these parts of speech by creating silly sentences.

What is important?

Priority Pyramid

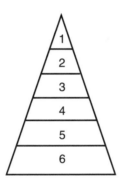

Students are asked to rank concepts by importance, (e.g., characters in a book, problem-solving strategies, food groups).

Your Ideas

What order?

Triangle Traverse

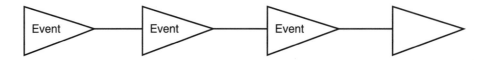

The students use sequencing skills to show the order of a story or of any activity that must be done in steps.

What is the cause?

The Arrow

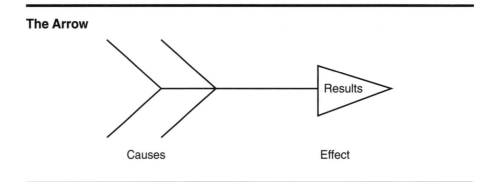

Students determine the causes for a particular result and write them on the "feathers." Or the teacher may write the causes and ask students to predict results.

How do I organize?

Files

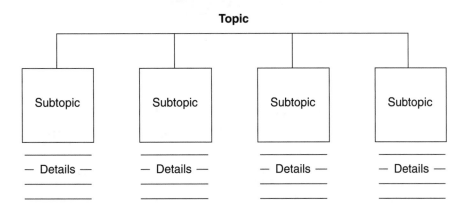

Students getting ready for a project or report may use "files" to set up the paper.

As you can see, graphic organizers are limited only by imagination. This student's "visible thinking" enhances his or her learning and recall.

PRIMARY SCHOOL

The Gathering Grid

Materials: A chart that introduces these vocabulary words: infer (to find out by reasoning; to use hidden clues to make a conclusion); gather (to collect); compare (to show how ideas or objects are alike); contrast (to show how objects or ideas are different); newsprint and markers for each group of three students or individual work sheets with a blank gathering grid.

Task: Divide the class into groups of three. Put a sample grid on the board or overhead. Above columns 1, 2, 4, and 5 insert the category names that the students will use. Above column 3, write the words: "likenesses." Brainstorm with the class ways the categories are alike in column 3. In the other column, brainstorm how each item is special. Note the completed example for presidents.

EXAMPLE: STUDENTS IN THE CLASS

AMY	LISA	STUDENTS	DAVE	CRAIG
blond	red	hair	brown	blond
blue	green	eyes	blue	brown
tall	tall	height	short	medium
reading	sports	hobbies	drawing	sports

After completing a sample with the whole class, provide a new grid for the students to complete in cooperative groups. Use material that the class is studying.

IRI/Skylight Publishing, Inc.

Reflection: Select several groups to share their completed grids with the whole class. After a group has shared its grid, ask the members to explain what they found easy and difficult about this task.

MIDDLE SCHOOL

What's in a Shape?

Materials: Provide each student pair with a work sheet. The pair will need one pencil.

Task: For this task, students use a Venn diagram to compare geometric shapes. On the board or overhead, show an example similar to this:

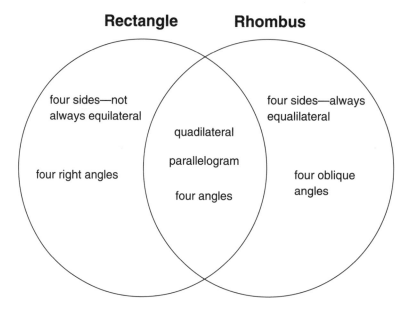

After you have shown this example, assign each group a different set of shapes to compare and contrast. Check the responses and then invite pairs to share their completed work. Post the Venns for all to see, or make copies for each pair to use in review study.

Reflection: Ask each student to think about how the Venn diagram helped him or her learn about geometric shapes. After the reflection, ask a volunteer to share his or her thoughts and record the response on the blackboard or overhead for all to see. Ask each student in turn to share his or her thoughts and put the responses on the board or overhead. If a student gives a response that is not clear to everyone, ask him or her to explain the answer. Finally, summarize all responses.

SECONDARY SCHOOL

African-American Innovators: A Study Matrix

Materials:

Give each trio of students a copy of the matrix form below, Famous Sports Figures.

Famous Sports Figures

Name	Sport	Team	Decade	Contribution

Task:

On the overhead or blackboard, show them how to use the matrix with this example. Have the class fill in the first column with names of sports figures they know. Fill in as much of the matrix as the class knows about. Ask them to explain where they could get the information for the cells they couldn't fill (e.g., magazines, encyclopedia, record books, biographies).

After the demonstration and a check to see that the groups know how to use a matrix, introduce the African-American innovators matrix and the materials the students will use. If the U.S. history text does not provide examples, assemble reading materials on the subject of major innovations made by African-Americans. Instruct the groups to identify the names of African-American innovators (e.g., Benjamin

Banneker, Rosa Parks, Daniel Hale Williams), and locate the information to fill in the century, issue, contribution, obstacles, and results columns. When the matrices are finished, ask each group to share what they found on one person.

African-American Innovators

Name	Century	Issue	Contribution	Obstacles	Results

Reflection: Assign the students to write a paragraph about the African-American innovators they researched. At the end of the paragraph, each student is to add several sentences explaining why he or she thinks it is important to know about these innovators.

IRI/Skylight Publishing, Inc.

Your Ideas

Multiple intelligences

Another theory in the "brain-compatible" universe is Howard Gardner's theory of multiple intelligences. Developed during Gardner's "Project Zero" research at Harvard, this theory begins with the assumption that I.Q. cannot adequately describe intelligence. Gardner (1983) identifies at least seven areas of human intelligence in which all people have varying degrees of strength. The seven intelligences have vast implications for instructional methods, which differ from the traditional, factory methods described earlier. Gardner describes the intelligences, as follows:

1 – Logical/mathematical intelligence

Logical/mathematical intelligence uses deductive or scientific reasoning. Persons with highly developed logical/mathematical reasoning tend to be good at problem solving and meeting challenges. These persons organize data, make observations, draw conclusions, recognize patterns, work with abstract symbols, and see connections between separate pieces of information. Occupations requiring this kind of intelligence are computer programming, mathematics, science, medicine, banking, and accounting.

2 – Bodily/kinesthetic intelligence

Persons who possess bodily/kinesthetic intelligence learn by physical experience. These individuals rely on tactile and kinesthetic experiences to internalize, understand, and retain information. They are generally good at activities which require physical performance, such as dance, drama, or physical education. These students take notes, not for the visual stimulation, but for the physical movement involved in writing. Unfortunately, hands-on learners are often neglected as they move into higher grade levels at school. Ninety percent of high school dropouts are kinesthetic learners. Bodily/kinesthetic occupations include dancing, acting, sports, physical education, and carpentry.

3 – Visual/spatial intelligence

Visual/spatial intelligence involves the use of space and perspective. The visual arts, including painting, drawing, and sculpture, are a part of this intelligence. It involves skills in visual discrimination, recognition, projection, imaging, and representing images. Children who daydream, doodle, and create fantasy stories and pictures are usually highly developed in visual/spatial intelligence. Artists, photographers, sculptors, and even some scientists use visual/spatial intelligence in their occupations.

4 – Musical/rhythmic intelligence

This intelligence includes the ability to recognize and use musical structures such as pitch, melody, rhythm, and timbre. Individuals with this intelligence are highly sensitive to sounds, such as music, noise, the human voice, and instruments. They may tap their pencils, feet, or fingers to rhythms unheard by others in the room. They easily learn information that is sung or set to a beat. Musicians, composers, conductors, and song- writers need musical intelligence in their occupations.

5 – Verbal/linguistic intelligence

Verbal/linguistic intelligence is the intelligence traditionally used in school. The SAT, ACT, and other standardized tests rely heavily on verbal/linguistic talent. Words and their meanings are the basis of verbal/linguistic intelligence. It involves comprehension, memory, recall, learning, and teaching through explanation. Verbal/linguistic occupations include teaching, news reporting, advertising, and writing.

6 – Interpersonal intelligence

Interpersonal intelligence involves the ability to work well with others. It involves the ability to form social relationships, to relate to others, to influence the thoughts and actions of others, and to adapt to different groups or situations. Politicians, counselors, mediators, social workers, and teachers use this type of intelligence in their professions.

7 – Intrapersonal intelligence

Intrapersonal intelligence involves internal knowledge of the self—of one's own thoughts and feelings. It includes the ability to relate inner thoughts and feelings to the outer experiences. Students with intraper-sonal intelligence tend to be self-motivated, independent, and goal-oriented. They may enjoy journal writing, thinking activities, and peer tutoring. Almost all helping professions require some degree of intrapersonal intelligence.

It is important for teachers to be aware that students may have strengths in some intelligences and weaknesses in others. This approach gives a very usable framework for thinking about new, learner-centered approaches for at-risk and dropout students. Over ninety percent of high school dropouts learn best through bodily/kinesthetic approaches. Yet traditional schools tend to emphasize only two of the intelligences: verbal/linguistic and logical/mathematical. Understanding that some students learn best visually, some auditorally, and some through taste, smell, touch or music, the teacher might plan activities using charts and diagrams (visuals). He or she might have students create a song or rap to teach the concept (auditory, bodily/kinesthetic, musical/rhythmic). By having students participate in a cooperative learning discussion group, the teacher has accessed the auditory and kinesthetic intelligences through the students' active involvement in the discussion.

IRI/Skylight Publishing, Inc.

Your Ideas

It doesn't always take major changes to use Gardner's theories. The easiest shift may involve merely a switch in language. For instance, different key words appeal to the different intelligences. By simply modifying the key phrase, the teacher can reach more students. For example, to the visual child, the question, "Do you see what I mean?" or "Do you get the picture?" would be meaningful. To the musical or auditory person, the question might be, "Can you hear what I'm saying?" or "Does that ring any bells for you?" The kinesthetic learner would respond better to, "Do you get a feel for what I'm saying?" In essence, the teacher has asked all the students the same question, "Do you understand?" By using different words, however, he or she communicates more effectively with more students. Though some students learn easily in the linear, sequential progression so familiar to schools, others learn in more global, right-brained ways, through images and stories. Since the mind constantly seeks patterns to give meaning to information, students who are addressed with language-specific questions are much more likely to discover the patterns that make learning relevant for them. The teacher's task is to provide the experiences that enable all children to learn and find meaning in their learning. Such structuring of the educational process can do a great deal to prove to educators that no one method of teaching will work for all students.

No teacher can take into account every variable for every student. But if the teacher knows how students input and process information, he or she can plan a variety of activities that offer more ways of learning than traditional lecture/note-taking methods.

Multiple intelligences can easily be addressed in most lessons if the teacher presents the lesson in a variety of ways. The following sample lessons incorporate Gardner's multiple intelligences.

PRIMARY SCHOOL

The Multiple Intelligences Story

Materials: None. However, the teacher should prepare a story using vivid, descriptive words.

Task: As the teacher tells or reads the story to the students (VL), they are asked to imagine (VS) themselves as an adverb or adjective. They are then asked to describe (VL) the feelings (Intra) they got as they became that part of speech (BK). Qualities of an adjective or adverb can be extracted from this exercise. Students who are reluctant to learn parts of speech seem to internalize the concepts more readily this way.

Intelligences: Verbal/Linguistic, Visual/Spatial, Intrapersonal, Bodily/Kinesthetic

Reflection: Students complete a PMI, answering the questions,
P (+) What were the pluses of this activity?
M (−) What were the minuses?
I (?) What did you find interesting?

MIDDLE SCHOOL

Fact Toss

Materials: Koosh ball.

Task: Students form a large circle (several smaller circles if the students are young) (BK). One person starts the activity by stating a fact (VL). (This can be review facts for social studies, science, times tables, addition, spelling, or anything that must be remembered). After stating his or her fact, the student names another person in the circle and tosses the ball to that person. The recipient of the ball thanks the thrower by name, introduces him- or herself, and states a new fact (VL, BK). He or she then tosses the ball to a different person in the circle, calling that person's name (Inter). After all students have had a turn, the teacher or a designated student points to a student in the circle, asking everyone else to remember his or her fact. This is repeated until everyone remembers everyone else's fact.

Intelligences: Bodily/Kinesthetic, Interpersonal, Verbal/Linguistic

Reflection: Students reflect on how this activity helped them recall information.

SECONDARY SCHOOL

Movement Machines

Materials: Access to films, videos, or real-life experiences, in which students are allowed to view movement in nature, art, and machines.

Task: After watching different types of movement, such as grasses, trees, and flowers moving in the wind; machines moving to complete a task; animals moving in nature; and performers moving in dance and theater (visual/spatial), students are asked to think of themselves individually as a machine (intrapersonal). Each student creates a movement machine (bodily/kinesthetic). Then in cooperative groups (interpersonal), students work together to create a movement machine.

Intelligences: Visual/Spatial, Intrapersonal, Bodily/Kinesthetic, Interpersonal

Reflection: Students reflect on the following questions: How did you contribute to the group? What might we do differently if we did this again?

Cooperative learning

Your Ideas

As discussed in the research chapter, the most critical brain-compatible strategy is cooperative learning. More than 500 studies have been conducted since 1900 concerning cooperative learning. Generally speaking, the studies have shown that cooperative learning results in greater:

- Motivation
- Involvement in learning
- On-task behavior
- Retention

And improved:

- Attitudes toward school
- Attitudes toward teachers
- Interpersonal skills
- Relationships with peers
- Higher-level reasoning

As might be expected, many teachers who read the literature and were trained in cooperative learning went back into their schools as "crusaders" for the cause. They spent every moment of every day in cooperative groups. Children and their parents and often even the teacher began to miss the individualization that many students needed to internalize new learning. Using cooperative learning exclusively became almost as boring as the straight rows of a few years ago. Balancing the types of classroom learning to match the children, the strategy, and the activity is the teacher's challenge.

Teachers typically structure learning in three ways: individualization, cooperation, or competition. Individual tasks might include work sheets, math problems, memorizing vocabulary, etc. Students function independently with no interaction.

Your Ideas

Competitive learning pits students against each other to see who's best. Most grading is done this way (the bell curve). School tasks tend to be competitive in some way—Who can get the most right? Who can finish first? Who can run fastest?

Cooperative activities place students in small groups to help each other master materials. Cooperative learning differs from simple group work, because cooperation includes creating a single product, requiring students to help each other, instructing students about social skills, and promoting positive interdependence within the activity.

Unfortunately, teachers tend to talk eighty percent of the school day. Most tasks require students to work quietly on their own. Passive rather than active learning is the norm. In the learner-centered classroom, cooperative learning should happen eighty percent of the time, with teacher talk limited to the other twenty percent. In this sense, cooperative learning is the foundation for a multitude of activities in learner-centered classrooms.

Cooperative learning need not always include long, formal tasks. At any time during a lesson, a teacher might:

1. Have student pairs describe what they notice about a topic.
2. Have student pairs explain important points to each other.
3. Have student pairs compare topics.
4. Ask students to list the qualities of or the rules for a topic.
5. Have cooperative pairs predict what would happen if. . . .
6. Let student pairs estimate results of. . . .
7. Have student pairs notice patterns.

Obviously, teachers have endless possibilities for less-than-five-minute activities for students to process important information. Groups of two or three students can be gathered and quickly dispersed. Such groups are spontaneous, less time consuming, and more actively interdependent than larger groups.

Often, cooperative learning activities encourage students to be positively interdependent upon each other. The teacher fosters interdependency by:

- assigning roles
- limiting materials
- jigsawing content
- holding the group accountable for all individuals' learning
- requiring the creation of one product
- structuring the environment to create group identity and norms

During the course of a day, a primary teacher might introduce a lesson with each child thinking about a question. "In this story, look at the pictures and predict what you think will happen." After students think alone, they can get into cooperative groups to compare ideas. Next, the teacher might read to the whole class and ask the groups to discuss how their predictions matched the story. He or she might conclude the activity with an all-class discussion before each child does a solo journal entry.

Because the business world demands workers to function as a team, it is increasingly important for teachers to teach cooperative skills.

Heterogeneous groups benefit student learning. However, they are not the only instructional arrangement. At times, such as when giving instructions, demonstrating a skill or procedure, summarizing lesson concepts, making transitions between lessons, and providing summary feedback, large-group instruction is most effective. At other times, homogeneous grouping or individualized study may be the most appropriate mode.

Homogeneous grouping is effective when it is necessary to review a concept or skill with a small of number of students, while others are able to proceed to advanced practice, lab work, or projects. For example, the teacher may form a temporary homogeneous group of students who need remedial help and provide them with direct instruction, while the others work in heterogeneous groups.

Homogeneous grouping and independent study may also occur when a small number of students master the core lesson concepts before the rest of the class. These students will benefit by working together on an advanced topic. Quite often, talented youngsters are ready to move from the understanding stage of learning to the application stage before their peers. Sometimes it is useful to have fast finishers tutor slower finishers in their groups. But sometimes fast finishers benefit from advanced challenges in a group of their peers or in independent study. If a classroom is truly learner-centered, all students will have the chance to work in a variety of grouping arrangements which most benefit their maximum learning potential.

PRIMARY
SCHOOL

Why Cooperate?

The teacher begins the lesson by explaining the importance of cooperation and asks students to think of a time when they worked well together. On a T-chart, they complete the "Looks like" and "Sounds like" for cooperation.

Example:

Looks Like	Sounds Like
heads together	one voice at a time
nods	soft voices
smiles	uh huh
one person's mouth moving at a time	that's a good idea
everyone doing a job	

Then the teacher asks students to think of a time when they did not cooperate, and they complete a T-chart for noncooperation.

Looks Like	Sounds Like
backs to each other	"That's my paper."
frowns	"Just shut up and let
people working alone	me work."

After explicit instruction in the social skills, the teacher reviews the consonant sounds the students will use for a language lesson. He or she then divides the class into groups of three. Roles are assigned.

The *materials person* gets an envelope containing cards with a consonant letter on each. Students walk around the room identifying objects that begin with the consonant sound. The *taper* tapes the letter on the object. The *reporter* tells the class what the object is and why it was chosen.

Reflection: Students reflect on how well their group cooperated and rate against the T-chart.

MIDDLE SCHOOL

State Symbols

In groups of four, students are given one piece of poster paper, writing paper, markers, and index cards. Each group chooses a state to research. The teacher assigns roles:

Recorder—Writes the information for the group in the report.

Artist—Draws the illustrations for the group.

KWL Charter—After the group comes to consensus on what they know and what they want to know about their state, the KWL charter records this information in columns on the index card.

K	W	L

Taskmaster—Makes sure each person has a part of the research to do. Makes sure the group is on task.

Students do research on their state, compile the information, produce a written report and illustrations, as needed, for the state bird, flag, flower, song, motto. The group may want to give oral presentations to the class as well as post their work on the walls.

Reflection: Students complete a PMI, stating what was a plus or a positive about this activity, what was a minus or negative aspect, and what was interesting.

P (+)
M (-)
I (?)

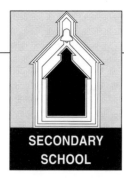

SECONDARY SCHOOL

All the World Is Our Stage

Secondary school literature students might be asked to read or listen to one of Shakespeare's plays. Groups of three or four are formed, with each person taking one part of the piece to read and interpret in a modern way. Members then join each other and jigsaw their portions to form a whole modern translation.

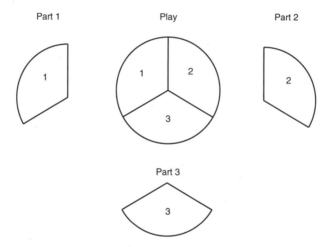

Reflection: In their journals, students complete the statements:

"I contributed to the group by. . . ."
"I received from the group. . . ."

In formal cooperative task groups, teachers structure the learning so that both content and interpersonal skills are taught, practiced, and debriefed as a part of every lesson. The teacher begins by giving subject area objectives and directions to the group. He or she then introduces a social skill to be emphasized during the lesson. At this time use of a T-chart may be helpful in the explicit instruction of the social skill. Finally, the teacher gives the jigsaw task instructions.

Cooperative Social Skills Lesson Example

The following are examples of social skills lessons appropriate for each level.

Your Ideas

Primary school level: Social skill – one person talks at a time

The teacher has students form circles of five. One child is chosen to be in the center as the listener. Students forming the circle all try to tell the middle student a story or a direction simultaneously. Different students take turns in the center. Students and teacher complete a triple T-chart:

Everyone Talks at Once

Looks Like	Sounds Like	Feels Like
center person looks at everyone confusion	noisy	uncomfortable can't hear

Then the activity is repeated, but each student takes turns talking. The center role is exchanged until everyone has a turn. Teacher and students then complete a triple T-chart.

One Person Talks at a Time

Looks Like	Sounds Like	Feels Like
student in center smiles happy	much more quiet	comfortable can hear

Your Ideas

Students reflect on the activity by responding to the following prompts:

When I did this activity I learned. . . .

Middle school level: Social skill – encouragement

The teacher begins the lesson by standing at the door of the classroom greeting each student with a smile, handshake, and positive comments as they enter the room. Students then form groups of three to discuss how they felt as they were greeted. Each student in the group generates two positive comments, one for each of the other group members. Group members share their positive comments. The teacher completes the T-chart using this experience to generate the description.

Encouragement

Looks Like	Sounds Like
smiles	I like . . .
heads nodding	That's a great idea . . .
learning together	

Students in the groups are then asked to think of a time when someone was discouraging. Each group member describes to the others how the incident made him or her feel. After the discussion, the teacher has students brainstorm ideas for the nonencouragement T-chart.

Nonencouragement

Looks Like	Sounds Like
frowns	sarcastic
leaning away	that's really a dumb
heads down	thing to do

Reflection: Students in groups respond to the following prompt:

Encouragement is important because. . . .

Closure: Students in their groups make chart board ads for encouragement and post them in the hallways.

Your Ideas

Secondary school level: Social skill – listening

Students need to find a partner and decide who will be A and who will be B. Partner A is directed to tell partner B something he or she would like for B to know. Partner B is told to do his or her best listening. At the end of thirty seconds, the teacher stops the activity and has the total group complete a T-chart for listening.

Listening

Looks Like	Sounds Like
eye contact	uh huh
nodding	yes
leaning toward	quiet

After generating as many responses as students can think of, the teacher has partner B tell partner A something he or she would like for A to know. Partner A's responsibility is to do everything possible NOT to listen to B with the exception of leaving the room. After thirty seconds, the teacher stops the activity and generates a T-chart.

Nonlistening

Looks Like	Sounds Like	Feels Like
no eye contact	coughing	frustrating
talking	laughing	unpleasant
looking away	talking	
walking away	noisy	

IRI/Skylight Publishing, Inc.

Reflection: In their journals, students complete: About listening, I feel. . . .

After teaching the specific social skill, the teacher gives directions for the content task the students are to perform. Students then carry out the objectives and activities specified by the teacher. The teacher moves from group to group facilitating the process. At the end of the activity, the teacher should debrief the content lesson (through the product, a test, explicit questions, etc.) and the interpersonal skill through group or individual reflection.

Thematic instruction

Another method of ensuring brain-compatible learning is thematic, integrated instruction.

Thematic instruction stems from the whole language philosophy of language arts instruction. Thematic units help students see patterns among content areas. Skills are not taught in isolation. Students use what they learn almost immediately.

The thematic approach appeals to the global learner, because it puts learning in context. Students get a broad perspective through the theme; they see the big picture rather than the smaller parts and find it easier to learn and remember information.

A commonly used approach to thematic, integrated instruction is the web (Fogarty, 1991). Typically, the web begins with an idea or theme as the central focus of all instruction. In self-contained classrooms, choosing themes is relatively easy. The challenge is greater when teams of teachers must come to consensus on meaningful themes. Choosing themes can generate dialogue among teachers that will help them set the curricular mastery guidelines for students.

The first step toward thematic or any integrated teaching begins with dialogue among teachers: first at their grade or developmental level, then with teachers from other grade levels. Teachers must decide what skills and habits are important for the age group they teach. They begin to see education in a broader sense, what comes before and what comes after their unit of time with the student (quarters, semesters, or years).

Using this model, teachers begin to see themselves as a link in the chain. These links are no longer isolated from one another but work together to establish the quality of the student's education. Teachers, perhaps for the first time, see themselves as part of a team, and they find the patterns in education that make the educational process meaningful to them. If a district or school has never given teachers time to dialogue, it should do so prior to any effort at implementation of thematic, integrated instruction. Teachers must become clear in their focus and mission if the school is to succeed. A curriculum guide or written plans are meaningless, unless the teachers take an active role and "buy in" to the mission of the school system. A dialogue is crucial in creating a lasting program.

The second step in creating a thematic approach to learning is for the teachers to examine their students—their developmental level, maturity, social skills, interests, and background—to decide upon a topic that will interest and motivate the students.

One difficulty in using the thematic approach is in selecting a theme. The theme must be broad enough to allow for meaningful instruction of several disciplines without seeming contrived or shallow. Too often teachers force instruction around themes such as "the circus" or "Halloween" and experience such difficulty making content fit the topic that they become discouraged and give up. A good theme should be generic yet interesting and meaningful, allowing for the diversities of the different

Your Ideas

IRI/Skylight Publishing, Inc.

*Your
Ideas*

disciplines. David Perkins calls these ideas "fertile themes." He establishes these criteria for fertile themes:

"Fertile themes for integrative learnings are like a good lens.

A good lens applies BROADLY,

A good lens applies PERVASIVELY,

A good lens discloses FUNDAMENTAL PATTERNS,

A good lens reveals SIMILARITIES AND
    CONTRASTS,

A good lens FASCINATES." (in Jacobs, 1989, p.70)

Of course, planning good themes requires a great deal of time and coordination among the team members. Initially, teachers may start with smaller, less comprehensive, and less time-consuming units. This helps teachers work into the model gradually and do it well.

Some of the concepts teachers report having success with in creating "fertile" thematic units are:

- Freedom
- Change
- Journeys
- Responsibility
- Friendship
- Cultures
- Diversity
- Patterns

Generally, teachers who are using a thematic approach use the web as a model for their plans. Starting with the central theme, the teacher webs different content areas or topics around the theme.

Multisubject Web

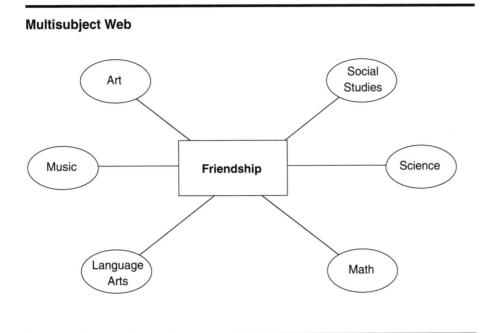

As you can see from the sample web, a teacher (or the students) may choose a fertile theme and develop subjects around the theme. Furthermore, each individual subject can be extended to form its own web.

Language Arts Web

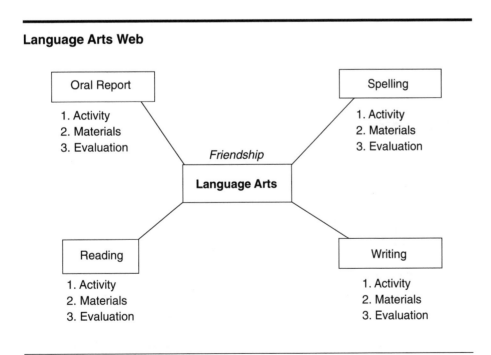

Your Ideas

The teacher can create a very detailed plan showing the specific goals, objectives, activities, materials, and assessments to be used.

An alternative might be to place a question in the center of the web and create a web that show the ways students might might go about finding the answers.

Investigation Web

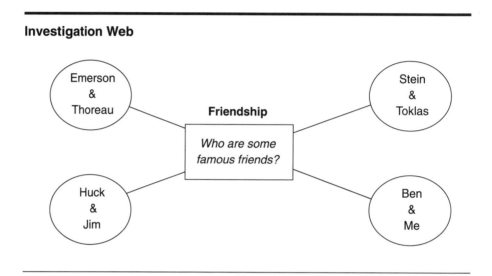

Under subtopics, cooperative groups or individuals might research and report about the topics. The ways teachers and students may use the web are limited only by their creativity. The web design should reflect what is most useful to the teacher and the team.

Whole language

"Whole language" is another brain-compatible philosophy of instruction well-suited to the learner-centered classroom. Whole language teachers believe that language instruction should not be fragmented. Skills are not taught in isolation but as meaningful tools to assist children in reading and comprehending relevant material.

The whole language teacher sees language as a tool for relating previous learning to new situations, helping students make sense of their world. Language components include listening, speaking, writing, and reading. All these components can be taught through interdisciplinary thematic units of instruction. The whole language teacher creates meaningful learning for students by carefully planning interesting units of study that allow individual children to explore and discover relationships among all the disciplines.

For example, a whole language teacher does not fragment his or her day into thirty- or fifty-minute segments of math, grammar, writing, science, social studies, etc. Rather, he or she plans instruction around central themes, such as patterns, freedom, conflict, etc. All subjects or disciplines might center around the topic of "patterns." The teacher would design various activities that would help students explore patterns in math, science, social studies, art, and English. Students might learn in small or large groups, in cooperative or individual settings. The teacher would explicitly teach and emphasize thinking skills believing that thinking is at the core of both reading and writing. To that end, in a whole language classroom books, newspapers, magazines, directories, signs, posters, samples of student writing, mailboxes for students to send and receive communications, writing centers, reading/library centers, research projects, games, listening stations, and other materials all contribute to a literate environment.

The teacher incorporates whole language philosophy. He or she creates a print-rich world where students are asked to perform meaningful tasks to solve real-life problems.

Primary school: Whole language

Whole language is the title most commonly given to a holistic, unfragmented philosophy of education. The predominant features of primary whole language are:

- Students are taught to read using trade books or literature rather than a contrived basal reader.

Your Ideas

IRI/Skylight Publishing, Inc.

Your Ideas

- Vocabulary and spelling lists come from the literature.
- Students write extensively; spelling is deemphasized; creativity of expression is encouraged.
- Stories and language experiences are posted on the walls to provide a print-rich environment.
- Students read and are read to daily.
- Independent reading is encouraged.
- Often metacognitive journals or learning logs are kept to validate learning experiences.
- Effort is taken to show the interconnectedness of all content (interdisciplinary units).
- Learning centers throughout the room offer students choices of activities to improve skills.
- Parents are asked to read to and with their children.

Middle School: Whole language

In the middle grades, comprehension and clarity becomes the focal points of language development. As students build on the foundations of reading started in the early grades, they welcome opportunities to become strategic learners across all the content areas. Likewise, they develop strong interest in communicating their ideas.

The Strategic Learner

A strategic learner purposefully chooses the learning strategies most appropriate for developing his knowledge and skills in each content area. Strategic learning begins when the student learns how to learn, not through memory, but through understanding of ideas.

The most effective and transferable learning strategies are the thinking tools that the student can adapt to different disciplines. Included in these are the graphic organizers (webs, Venns, matrices, etc.) and mnemonics (word patterns). These devices, each attuned to a specific thinking pattern, enable the student to organize and process information, especially print information, in meaningful ways. (Bellanca, 1991). Thus, after students learn to use graphic organizers and mnemonics with easy material, they can use them to gather more complex information from their reading materials. Next, they organize the information according to specific cognitive functions (compare, analyze, synthesize) in preparation for a writing task.

In a similar manner, graphic organizers help students listen for thoughtful content, analyze the speaker's intentions and assess purpose. When used for thought processing, the organizers highlight relationships and connections among different topics and contents. From the organizers spring multiple opportunities to enhance reading, writing, speaking and listening.

Secondary school: Whole language

Much of secondary school curricula isolates subject matter. Therefore, secondary school students develop decisive attitudes about their subjects—"English is not history." "Science is not math." "Why do we have to write in business class?"

The whole language philosophy in secondary school starts with reading and writing across the curricula. Although writing and reading instruction begin in the English classroom, every teacher can reinforce language development by adhering to standards of grammar and sentence usage by assigning essays and research papers, and by using journals and logs for reflective writing assignments.

All teachers can also develop students reading abilities in the respective content areas. This can be done through advanced graphic organizers appropriate to the subject areas. For instance, the matrix and the Venn make excellent study tools in science. Students can compare and contrast different species they are studying. As

Your Ideas

*Your
Ideas*

they observe differences, students can use the matrix to organize and detail what they see. Similarly, in English, the students can use the same tools for comparing characters in a short story. In social studies they can compare cultures or historic periods. As the students become more skilled in using graphic organizers, the teacher can mediate how well the students are thinking and problem solving.

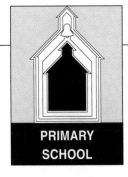

PRIMARY SCHOOL

Classroom News

Background: Writing activities help students learn how to write well *and* how to read better. Growth in reading and writing is interdependent; so writing should become an important part of the day's activities. A class journal or news chart allows the teacher to model writing for students in a relevant format.

Materials: Large chart paper, markers.

Task: The teacher gathers the students in a tight group, allowing every student to see the chart. He or she begins the writing with dialogue similar to the following:

> T: Who can tell me what today is?
> S: Tuesday
> T: Who knows what the word Tuesday begins with?
> S: T
> T: Can you hear any other letters in the word? (Teacher fills in letters students do not know.)
> T: What do we leave before our next word?
> S: Space
> T: Now, what does our class want to write about today?

After students choose a topic, the teacher elicits sentences from them and writes them on the chart. Students and teacher read the article together.

Articles may be hung around the room each week and reviewed daily, and they may be compiled into a newsletter to be sent home to parents as a part of the student's portfolio.

IRI/Skylight Publishing, Inc.

Reflection: Ask students to respond to these questions: What did you learn about writing? How can what you learned help you with future news stories?

MIDDLE SCHOOL

It's in the Pocket

Background: Teachers often have difficulty getting middle grade students to write content-related reports without "just copying" the reference books. This activity may help students use references without copying them.

Materials: Pocket chart and index cards.

Task: Using commercially-made or teacher-made pocket chart*, have students brainstorm questions about their report topic. For example, if the report topic is volcanoes, students might want to know:

What is a volcano?
What are some famous volcanoes?
What causes volcanoes to erupt?

After generating a list of questions, students are placed in cooperative groups. Each group is given one or two questions to research.

The question for each group is placed at the top of the pocket chart. Down the left-hand side, students generate a list of places they might look for this information, such as magazines, books, encyclopedias, etc. Each student in the group takes several index cards to the library and using one of the reference sources from the chart, reads to find the information. For example, a student might be using magazines to answer the question, "Where are some famous volcanoes?"

while another student in the group uses encyclopedias to answer the same question. Information is written on index cards and placed in the pocket chart. When all groups have their cards in place, the teacher can pull all index cards dealing with each topic, give them to a group, and have the group write a paragraph (or page) on that topic. The various topics can be linked together to form one cohesive report that is written by students instead of copied from the encyclopedia.

*Pocket chart
Pocket charts can be made by affixing library pockets in rows across poster paper. The references can be filled in permanently or taped on for each project. See example.

Volcanoes			
References	**What are they?**	**Why do they erupt?**	**What are some famous ones?**
encyclopedia			
books			
magazines			
videos			
filmstrips			

index card

pocket

Reflection: Have students think about how the chart could help them organize other studies.

IRI/Skylight Publishing, Inc.

SECONDARY SCHOOL

Enacting History

Background: In the traditional secondary school, the mailbox curriculum makes it hard for teachers to imagine using the whole language philosophy. As in the other grades, the learner-centered teacher can integrate reading, writing, and speaking with thinking as the core theme.

Materials: Student-made costumes, journals, student-made play settings.

Task: Start this project with mixed ability and grade level students. The outcomes will be a journal about the steps of the project, the students' learnings, and an assessment of the project's worth; a summary of the research; the script; and the enactment of a simulated historic decision, (speaking). Have student groups research a significant historic event and prepare an authentic reenactment. Each group will present its play to the class in authentic costume. For example, the incident is the first informal cabinet meeting held after Lincoln's assassination. The group members will play the roles in costume of the cabinet members their research showed present. The students must write their own dialogue as they imagine it might have been.

Reflection: Make a pro-con T-chart for journals. Have groups assess their enactments and write their pros and cons.

How do we evaluate in the learner-centered classroom?

Authentic assessment

Authentic assessment without standards, curricular frameworks, and new teaching methods is impossible. Brain-compatible teaching requires brain-compatible assessment. Note the use of the word *assessment* versus the traditional term *testing*. Assessment implies multiple indicators and sources of evidence taken over time rather than a one-time, one-format method of judging skills. Tests, interviews, surveys, and projects are all a part of assessment. Assessment is the big picture.

Authentic assessment answers these questions: What do they know? How do we know what they know? As educators become more knowledgeable of the assessment process, they have realized that traditional standardized

IRI/Skylight Publishing, Inc.

test scores do not measure significant learner performances. Rather, these tests tend to measure achievement and performance of skills at one particular moment in time. Poor test takers know that test anxiety, or other conflicting emotional states, can affect standardized test scores negatively. Research consistently demonstrates that overreliance on standardized testing harms many students; yet parents and the general public tend to judge the schools by the standardized test scores that are published in the paper.

Why is this practice still carried out in every state? Why are parents and community so accepting of these scores? The answers tend to be complex. For many parents, test scores are the only objective results they see all year. Teachers, seldom trained to write tests, have a poor reputation for test-making skills. Many parents do not trust the teacher-made tests given throughout the year. Teachers are not usually required to take courses in evaluation and assessment as part of their coursework for graduation. Once they are hired, teachers are thrust into the role of test maker and student evaluator, but little inservice is given in development of assessment techniques. Teacher-made tests may be ambiguous, shallow, or unfair. But without instruction, coaching, and support to create more valid items, there is little chance for improvement in test design. Hill (1990) also criticizes teachers who allow discipline to enter into assessment. Students are given Fs or zeroes for not bringing supplies, homework, or signed papers to class.

Authentic assessment is true to its name—authentic. Authentic assessment includes different types of data-gathering technique and consistently evaluates the total student, rather than isolated "snapshots" of the student. The possibilities for gathering data are endless and limited only by the creativity of the teacher. Performances, projects, portfolios, teacher-made tests, writing samples, and observation check lists are all a part of a teacher's options for looking at the total student. Teachers who value mastery rather than the bell curve tend to use the more authentic measures to assess progress. They are not as much interested in comparing each child to other children as they are with ensuring that every child has the knowledge and skills necessary to succeed.

Your Ideas

What are the basic tools?

Observation check lists

Observation, the most common of the assessment tools, is the oldest and one of the most useful in a variety of learning activities. It works well for science, math, sports, music, or other fine arts performances—from the mundane to the extraordinary. Observation done well with specific goals can provide data for assessing needed skills.

Specific and objective observation of authentic learning involving higher-order thinking skills can be done through a check list of behaviors. When a teacher observes a behavior, he or she either puts a tally mark or a check to indicate its occurrence. Frequency of the behavior can be ascertained by making tally marks each time the behavior is observed. Check lists can be designed either for individuals or for groups of students working together on a project. For example, a teacher may be assessing the student's problem-solving behavior. Using the T-chart established by the students, the teacher looks for the tell-tale behaviors.

Your Ideas

Problem Solving

	Plans Problem-Solving Steps	Checks Steps Taken	Explores Optional Steps
Johnny	II	I	
Joan	I	I	
Susan		I	I
Jim		I	

or

	Plans Problem-Solving Steps	Checks Steps Taken	Explores Optional Steps
Group A	IIII	II	III
Group B	II	IIII	I
Group C	III	I	III

When students see the charts, they begin to see specific ways to control their own behavior. Similar check lists might be used for listening skills, organizational skills, types of questions missed on a test, or elements of skillful performance.

Rating scales

The major obstacle teachers encounter with the observation/oral report is making it objective so that parents and other teachers and the student understand the criteria and how the criteria is evaluated. A student making an oral presentation might be scored on:

> Content
> Delivery (volume/pitch/tone)
> Clarity
> Organization

For each, the teacher would need to establish a rubric to indicate what the student must do in order to achieve maximum points. With each rubric, the teacher would provide a rating scale. For instance, for oral presentation "content," the teacher could scale "accuracy" and "appropriate information."

Selects appropriate information.

0	3	5
too little	adequate	great

Covers content accurately.

0	3	5
many mistakes	some mistakes	few, if any, mistakes

By setting up the criteria in this way, both the students and the observers can easily view and understand the elements of the presentation that *were* strong and those that *were* weak. More important, they make assessment of student performances much easier. Under each Likert, the observer can jot down examples or reasons for the rating.

What strategies encourage authentic performances?

Art work/illustrations
Students with strong visual/spatial intelligence can demonstrate their skills through illustrations or other art forms. Illustrations are a very useful measure of students' understanding and ability to conceptualize information.

As with oral projects and observations, the teacher must clearly explain the criteria and indicators of success. This makes the assessment relevant to students and parents.

*Your
Ideas*

Artifacts

Anything a student produces as a result of his or her acquisition of knowledge can be an assessment item. Students can show varying degrees of sophistication in the type and quality of product developed as a project.

Creating an artifact such as a video, collage, play, sculpture, mobile, map, collection of poems, machine, computer program, or book requires a transfer of knowledge into application. Criteria check lists and scales help students apply knowledge and meet quality standards.

Oral/written reports

As students advance from invented spelling and "author's chair" storytelling to formal essay writing and creative short stories, rubrics that describe the criteria for success enable the students to internalize standards of excellence and do their own self-assessments.

In addition to the completion of the oral or written assignment, inviting students to turn in their own check lists or written self-evaluations enriches their learning.

**Sample
Check List**

Self-Assessment Check List

1. _____ correct spelling
2. _____ correct grammar
3. _____ introduction of important ideas
4. _____ middle paragraphs
5. _____ summary paragraphs
6. _____ clear examples
7. _____ use of metaphor

Written Self-Assessment

1. In this essay, I am intending to improve. . . .

2. What I did best was. . . .

IRI/Skylight Publishing, Inc.

Portfolios

The easiest way to think of portfolio assessment is to imagine a great file cabinet. Inside the cabinet are multitudes of files in different drawers. Each file may contain evidence of learning; each drawer may vary. One drawer may be for written work, one for media, one for projects, one for oral work, art work, etc. Each drawer contains files. Files in the art work drawer might include collages, murals, comic strips, drawings, or crafts. Teaching students how to organize their material in a portfolio promotes their thinking skills. It also allows the teacher to have a "whole picture" to evaluate and to communicate to parents.

In the learner-centered school, the portfolio can be the centerpiece of each learner's personal history of learning. In the primary grades, the portfolio is most valuable to teachers, students, and parents if it is kept at two levels. At level one, the portfolio is a day-by-day, week-by-week collection of the student's best work across the curriculum. At the beginning of each year, the student can divide the portfolio into sections based on annual learning goals. These goals are established in a parent-teacher-child conference in the first month. As the student completes tasks each week, he or she selects the artifacts (tests, observation sheets, essays, art products, performances, etc.) that best meet the criteria for excellence or the criteria for personal improvement. After four to six weeks, the child selects those works which he or she believes show his or her best performances and shares these in conference with his or her parents and teacher. At the end of the school year, the student does a final culling of the best material for the year and presents these in a conference with a selection rationale based on the goals set at the year's start.

At the second level, primary students maintain a master portfolio that includes only the best work for each calendar year. This portfolio is kept in the principal's

Your Ideas

record room. As the student reviews each year, he or she can look back on previous development and chart progress over several years.

Teachers can plan for each student to keep a single portfolio, even when he or she may have several different areas of study to include. The process is the same as in the lower grades.

1. The student sets goals and selects criteria for pinpointing his or her personal best work.
2. At short intervals, the student selects the work to retain and provides reasons based on criteria and goals.
3. At quarter or semester breaks in the year, the student increases the selectivity and confers with parents and/or teacher on his or her accomplishments during that period.
4. At the end of each year, the student makes a final selection of best work according to his or her criteria and goals and summarizes progress during that year.
5. If grades are required, the teacher completes a rubric-based assessment with criteria detailed on a Likert scale and closes the portfolio with a letter grade.
6. At least one annual conference should take place among the student, teacher, and parent. If a conference is not possible, the student should share the portfolio with his or her parents after the teacher has added comments about the student's progress, as shown in the portfolio.

The challenge for a teacher in setting up the learner-centered portfolio is to determine what artifacts or products to have students include. If the teacher has been careful to set up the authentic criteria that Archbald and Newmann (1988) suggested and the teacher assists each student in setting realistic learning goals, the list of what to include becomes matter of fact. Kay Burke (1993) has a "short list" of twenty-eight items that experienced teachers could easily expand.

Your Ideas

1. Homework
2. Teacher-made quizzes and tests
3. Peer editing assignments
4. Group work (artifacts or pictures)
5. Learning logs
6. Problem-solving logs
7. Reflective journals
8. Community projects
9. Written work
10. Rough drafts of written work to show process
11. Cassettes of speeches, readings, singing, questioning techniques
12. Graphic organizers
13. Questions for a conference
14. Questionnaires about attitudes and opinions
15. Interviews with other students
16. Observation checklists
17. Metacognitive activities
18. Self-assessments
19. Letter to teacher or parents about contents of portfolio
20. Statement of future goals
21. Free pick (no criteria given)
22. Pictures of performances such as speeches, plays, debates, historical re-enactments
23. Pictures of individual projects or group projects that are too big to include
24. A registry or log where students date and discuss when and why they log in an entry and when they take out an entry
25. Computer programs
26. Lab experiments
27. Samples of artwork (or pictures)
28. Videos of performances

Burke (1993, p. 47–48)

IRI/Skylight Publishing, Inc.

If the portfolio is based on each student's learning goals, the student's self- assessment, and the student's dialogue with parents, the portfolio becomes a key tool in forming a learner-centered classroom. Time spent helping the student form goals, identify criteria, select learning methods, accept teacher feedback, assess personal performance, and share results with significant others is not time lost or time added to the cramped curriculum. It is valuable time allotted in each day, week, and month that provides a framework for each learner's construction of meaning from the curriculum. Considering how learning occurs, it is the most important time that each student will spend in transforming the curriculum into personal accomplishments.

Establishing rubrics for learner-centered performances

In the '70s, teachers revolted against the use of grades. Computer-based report cards, mastery learning check sheets, written evaluations, and other alternatives were attempted. The move to replace grades gave way to the "back-to-the-basics" movement of the '80s. Influenced by the many calls to reform curriculum in the '90s, the concerns about grades emerged, albeit in a different form.

The most recent calls for reform of student evaluation go far deeper than the concern for the detrimental effects of grades. These calls arise from a recognition that single-answer tests and letter grades do not fit well with the learner-centered approach. Rather than using tests as the sole tool for evaluating a student's capabilities, the reformers are calling for multiple assessments of student performance. Ferrara and McTighe (1992, p. 338) compare this approach to the making of a motion picture— using many scenes, angles, and points of view to review a student's learning life. This contrasts with the old single-photo shot—using a test or grades to determine learning.

Selectivity is at the heart of the assessment process advocated for learner-centered classrooms. Therefore, Burke (1993) and others call for the creation of classroom-centered rubrics. A rubric is a framework of performance standards, criteria, and success indicators used by a student or teacher to measure the student's learning performance. While acknowledging the value of national and state standards that enable comparisons of state and national performance, Burke (1993) and Chapman, Swartz, and Bellanca (1994) assert that each teacher should have the opportunity and the support to customize rubrics to their own classrooms. In this way, classroom teachers can honor the expectation of state standards, but maintain the integrity of the learner-centered classroom.

In a number of states, such as New York and Minnesota, standards do not have to be reinvented. These states' legislatures have set high standards compatible with the learner-centered classroom. What the learner-centered teacher can do is select and target standards that fit with the goals of his or her students and tailor the rubric to guide assessment.

For instance, in New York's mandated *A New Compact for Learning*, a number of standards relate to the promotion of higher-order thinking. Having selected one of those standards, the teacher, or a grade-level team, can frame within fifteen minutes a very usable rubric for a learner-centered classroom. There is no need for elaborate district or school teams to spend hours writing complex rubrics that have little value to students or teachers.

Here is an example of a complex thinking rubric. This rubric outline contains all the needed elements: the standard, the criteria, and the indicators of success.

*Your
Ideas*

THE RUBRIC

Standard: Developing Rhythm

CRITERIA

High Performance: Student can arrange words to fit a rhythmical pattern
    Indicators: Word pattern makes sense
                Word sequence has an identifiable rhythm/pattern
                Pattern fits all words

Sound Performance: Student can fit words to pattern given by teacher
    Indicators: Student hears pattern
                Student arranges words to fit pattern

Adequate Performance: Students can follow song pattern lead by teacher
    Indicators: Students identify pattern lead by teacher
                Students keep the pattern

Not Yet: No beat
    Indicators: Student cannot hear pattern
                Student cannot keep pattern

(Bellanca, Chapman and Swartz 1994, p. 92)

Follow these guidelines when constructing a learner-centered rubric:

1. Select standards that can be adapted to the students in your classroom.
2. Share the rubrics with students. Discuss the vocabulary and encourage students to review the rubric before starting a performance.
3. Be sure that the rubric will challenge all students to do their best work.
4. Encourage self-assessment of performances with the rubric.
5. Avoid using letter or number grades as the only tool for reporting student progress. If possible, replace report cards with parent-teacher-student conferences that review an entire portfolio.

If the teacher who made this rubric were not required by his or her district to provide letter grades, no grades would be scaled for the indicators or criteria. In place of grades, the students and the teacher would check the indicators reflecting the students' work. Artifacts in the portfolio which relate to the indicator would be numbered for easier matching with the indicator list. During parent-teacher-student conferences, students would be asked to explain how they assessed their work with this rubric as a guide.

Your Ideas

If a teacher were required to attach a letter grade to the portfolio work, he or she might:

1. Give a point value to each indicator. Add up the points on each artifact via a performance scale matched to the criteria (5 points = adequate, 8 points = strong, 12 points = high). Total all points earned for each indicator and assign a grade (10 = C, 20 = B, 30 = A) based on the total indicator score.

2. Using a scale, give a point value to each artifact (e.g., 1 = low through 5 = high). Total the artifact scores and assign a letter grade to each performance level (Adequate = C, Strong = B, High = A).

Make your own

Take a moment to think about a lesson or concept you teach every year. How could you structure your lesson using a rubric? Create your own rubric.

YOUR RUBRIC

   Standard:

                           CRITERIA

   High Performance:
     Indicators:

   Sound Performance:
     Indicators:

   Adequate Performance:
     Indicators:

   Not Yet:
     Indicators:

IRI/Skylight Publishing, Inc.

What is the parent's role in the learner-centered school?

No program or school can be totally successful without parent involvement. Because parents are such an essential element in the learner-centered classroom, we have dedicated a separate section to assist teachers in getting parents involved in the school.

In the traditional classroom, the roles of the teacher and parent have often been adversarial. The teacher may come to the conference table, grade book in hand, somewhat defensive, and expecting an unpleasant interview. The parent, too, comes to school with a defensive attitude. Both teacher and parent fear that they will be found inadequate in their roles. Is it any wonder that so many parent-teacher conferences are unpleasant since both come to the meeting feeling defensive? Unfortunately,

IRI/Skylight Publishing, Inc.

the parent-teacher conference symbolizes how the relationships in the entire organization function. It is essential for teachers to learn to communicate well with parents.

Involving parents of primary students

The primary parent kit

One way of boosting communication for many teachers to establish a "parent kit." The kit comprises ideas and suggestions for parents that will help their children perform better in school. The following might be incorporated into the kit:

1. Suggestion cards. Write a suggested activity/method that parents can help their children with on an index card. Cards can be laminated and sent home daily, or the teacher may prefer to send the information as a newsletter. The cards might include these:

   - Keep your child healthy. Check vision/hearing regularly.
   - Make sure your child has breakfast.
   - Set a bedtime schedule and stick to it.
   - Read the cereal box with your child.
   - Read road signs with your child.
   - Have your child sort and count socks/silverware.
   - Talk with your child. Don't just ask "What did you do in school today?" Ask about what he or she has learned. Ask to see samples of writing, etc. Ask your child to read to you for ten minutes.
   - When listening to your child read, stop at the end of each page (or few pages) and ask for a summary of what he or she has just read. Then ask for a prediction about what might happen next.
   - Let your child record him- or herself reading and play the recording as you drive to work.

IRI/Skylight Publishing, Inc.

- Have your child read a recipe to you as you cook (older children can measure and help prepare).
- Allow your child to help sort and put away groceries. Ask him or her to explain why certain items are grouped together.
- Have your child look for patterns throughout the house and yard. Let him or her record these patterns on a wall chart. For example, he or she looks on the mantle and sees a candlestick, a picture and a candlestick, and on a bookshelf he or she sees a flower, a flower and a book. The wall chart might look like this:

candlestick	picture	candlestick
A	B	A

flower	flower	book
A	A	B

- Read to your child. Stop periodically and ask him or her to summarize and/or predict what will happen next.
- Play a home version of "Hide in Plain Sight" by taking a toy or stuffed animal and moving it daily until the child guesses the "hidden" object.

Children in a primary class can rotate through the cards, taking a different one home every two to three nights. When the parent returns the card (signed), the student gets a new card.

2. A take-home computer for students to practice on.
3. Books of appropriate levels for students to read.
4. Puzzles for parents to complete with their children.
5. Books created at school by the students.
6. Simple science experiments that can be performed in the kitchen.
7. Maps with places you can help your children find.

Your Ideas

Your Ideas

The parent kit enables parents who work and cannot volunteer at the school to feel they are a part of their children's education. It keeps them informed and involved with the classroom. Parents who work can also be involved in volunteer work that doesn't require being there. They may, for example:

- Assist in correcting papers,
- Operate a homework hotline for students at night, or
- Provide resources for classroom projects.

For parents fortunate enough to be able to volunteer during the day, they can:

- Read to students in groups or individually.
- Listen to students. Parents can listen to individual students read or recite their multiplication tables or any other practice the teacher suggests.
- Be research guides—Parents take students in small groups to the media center where they may do research or learn library skills.
- Help in textbook/unit planning—Parents who are interested in curriculum might be invited to sit on textbook or thematic unit planning committees. This empowers parents and creates better communication of the school's goals between home and school.
- Join the advisory/leadership committee—Parents might be invited to join in the school's leadership (research and development) team. Their input into the school's vision is extremely important if they are to support the school.
- Be chaperones/drivers—Often parents who are able to volunteer a part of their day to the school can perform a vital role by chaperoning and driving students on field trips, etc.

A word about middle school

Middle School, that strange age between elementary and high school, can pull parent volunteer activities from both elementary and high school, although high school activities tend to work best. However there are a few unique parent activities for middle school that can be applied only to that age. A few suggestions for parent activities are listed below.

Transition team

Parents can form groups to help ensure the smooth and successful passage of students from elementary to middle school. These parents may provide orientation for students by having teachers, administrators, parents or counselors visit the elementary school to discuss middle school programs and answer questions. These orientation sessions seem to help the students adjust to the change.

Transition week

The first week at the middle school can be traumatic. Parent volunteers on campus can assist students with opening lockers, finding classes, following procedures, and any other problems students may encounter.

Orientation night

Parents can sponsor an orientation night at the middle school for both students and parents. The program might include a welcome from administrators and counselors, a tour of the facility, introduction to middle school courses and procedures, and other information helpful to new students.

Orientation for parents

A separate night of orientation should be provided for parents to acquaint them with middle school routines, goals and procedures. At this time, parents can have their questions and concerns answered prior to beginning the new year.

IRI/Skylight Publishing, Inc.

Your Ideas

High school transition

When middle grade students reach their last year at the middle level, usually eighth grade; counselors, teachers, and administrators from the high school may want to provide an orientation to high school. Students can be taken to the high school to see the layout. They also can be given a handbook and have routines and procedures explained to them.

Preregistration

When middle school students are ready to go to high school, frequently a preregistration is held. The counselors usually provide the preregistration forms and go into the classrooms to explain options, graduation requirements, etc. This is a good time for the counselor to provide career counseling, letting students know which occupations require which degrees of education. Parents can assist by attending, by assisting the counselor and by carefully studying graduation requirements to ensure that their student graduates.

Of course the examples of parent involvement programs listed above are a few of the many available. Some of the elementary ideas are applicable as well as some of the high school. It is important to remember that parent involvement at this age is likely to drop off due to the student's struggle for independence. But it is also a crucial time for parents to stay involved. We, as educators, need to ask, ask, and ask parents to participate in our programs if our schools are to succeed.

Involving parents at the high school level

Parental involvement at the high school level may pose quite a challenge for both the school and parent. Students at this stage of development are trying to break free of their dependence on parents (and other adult authority

IRI/Skylight Publishing, Inc.

Your Ideas

figures) and may impede communication between home and school. Therefore, a different approach to parental involvement may become necessary. Rather than directly volunteering within the student's classes, parents may become involved in more school-wide and district activities. Parental involvement at this age is just as important to effective schools as at the elementary and middle school levels. This is no time to "give up" on parents. Some of the best volunteer programs in the nation are conducted at the high school level. Below are described some ideas for high school parent involvement that have been shown to be effective.

Academic booster clubs

Academic boosters began as an offshoot of band and athletic boosters, and generally comprises parents of students who perform well in school. They may assist in BETA club, academic activities, and trips, search for scholarships, assist students in drama, debate, or other academic programs. These parents generally want to serve on school and district curriculum committees. They are a valuable addition to school committees designed to set the goals for the school. They may assist with setting up volunteer programs, with studying curriculum and texts to determine the best for their school, with career days, job shadowing, adopt-a-school programs, teacher appreciation days, etc. They help to establish the standards for the school and ultimately for the district and state. Academic Boosters are involved in many of the school's support activities such as:

1. Homework hotline: This practice, begun at elementary level is creeping slowly into high school practice. Many parents who can not volunteer time during the regular school day can give a couple of hours per week at night to assist students having difficulty with some aspect of their homework. With enough volunteers, parents only need to give up 1 to 2 hours every other week to

*Your
Ideas*

have a successful program. Call forwarding makes it possible for students to have *one* easy to remember number to call.

2. Parents are also involved in activities designed to raise SATs: Students can take home computer software and have parents help them work on raising SAT scores. Trial tests developed by the school counselors can help parents determine their child's need for assistance.

Parent volunteer pool directory

Survey parents early in the year to see which parents might be available for classroom presentations or to have students visit their work place on study trip or perhaps to volunteer services. This resource directory need not be limited to just parents. Community businesses like to get involved also. Parents and other community members may be kept in a reference directory which indicate categories of services offered by the volunteers. A brief description of what the volunteer is willing to do could follow each listing, enabling teachers to match their need to community resources. The list is limited only by the imagination. Volunteers might:

• Speak on various topics
• Allow students to visit their place of work
• Allow job shadowing
• Tutor remedial students
• Volunteer for the office
• Grade papers
• Drive for field trips
• Participate in career day
• Offer interest inventories
• Judge contests such as science/social studies fairs

Adopt-a-school

Frequently this is thought of as only businesses offering money or services to schools. It need not be that way. Sometimes a neighborhood might adopt a school and

IRI/Skylight Publishing, Inc.

provide volunteer tutors on a rotational basis. Any parent or group of parents can adopt the school and provide services.

Parents who adopt a school may be similar to academic boosters although that is not necessarily the case. These adoptive parents may help the school solicit money from philanthropic persons or groups to implement new programs. For example, they might solicit money to train teachers in Reuven Feuerstein's Instrumental Enrichment, a program proven to be especially successful at risk or special needs intermediate, middle and high school students.

Your Ideas

Tutorial assistance in instruction

With as many bilingual students as we have in our schools, teachers can use all the help they can get in the bilingual and regular classes. Having parents who can assist in interpreting and tutoring these students is a real help to the school.

Back to school

In some high schools particularly ones with high drop-out rates and low percentages of parents who finished high school, administrators are allowing parents to come back to school to finish their degree. Although they are placed in different classes from their children, the parents seem to exert a positive effect on the entire school. Discipline improves and more homework gets done!

Involvement planned performances

The best way to get parents to school is to plan a performance or assembly in which their student will participate. This allows the parents to become involved and get to know the school and teachers on an informal basis. It encourages parents to continue their involvement with the school and makes them less apprehensive when there is a problem that requires them to come to school.

Parents helping parents

Every school should have a place where parents can come and relax as they volunteer. If the teachers lounge is unavailable to parents, there should be some room set aside, manned by volunteer parents. This room might serve as an informal lounge or it might become a resource center for parents. Parents could visit the lounge when they have school related questions or problems and find answers from other parents. Additionally this room could serve as the Leadership Team room once a week for informal school/parent meetings. These meetings are described under the "Leadership team hour."

Leadership team hour

Once a week the principal should make him- or herself available for an open forum with parents. These meetings should be informal with "coffee and donuts" to allow parents to express concerns or ask questions. Many administrators fear that these sessions might become "gripe" sessions but with a little conflict resolution training this problem can usually be avoided. It is well worth the effort.

Workshops and courses for parents

Often parents want to assist their students but do not know how. Counselors and teachers can assist by providing workshops for parents. Topics might include: applying to college, SAT preparation, scholarship information, career decision making, how to help without yelling, etc.

These workshops can also provide basic skills training for parents. This may be the key to getting low income parents of "at risk" students involved in the school. Teaching them basic skills so they can help their children is providing a service to them as well as the school.

Advocacy groups

Parents who want real decision making power and who have the time to devote to it should be encouraged to sit

Your Ideas

on district and state planning committees. It will be much easier to gain the support of the community for new programs if parents have been involved. Too often only the parents of high achievers become members of advocacy groups. The parents of low achievers tend to "get lost." Thus their students are not well represented and tend to get less advantages than others. Administrators and teachers excuse this lack of representation by claiming that these parents do not volunteer. This is true but is no excuse. Many inner city schools have high volunteer rates. If asked how they accomplish this, they will tell you they ask, they pursue, they ask, they ask, they ask. It is imperative we seek out these parents and involve them.

Obviously, it is impossible to list all of the possibilities for parent involvement at the high school level. The important aspect of a parent involvement program is getting it started well. The ultimate goal is to have a comprehensive plan with all the components spelled out specifically. A method of assessing the success of each component must be included, and a plan of action for each component must be described in terms of the benefits to teachers, parents, and students. With relevant parent activities and strong support from the principal, a parent involvement program at any level is bound to meet with success.

Parental involvement can make or break a school. It is important for teachers to remember that they do not teach in isolation; the home and community are also a large part of the child's life. If schools are to succeed, parents and community must be involved. Many will become involved if the teacher creates a warm and welcoming climate, if the parents feel valued, and if they believe they are empowered as real working members of the school's programs and can help make decisions that will improve education for their children.

IRI/Skylight Publishing, Inc.

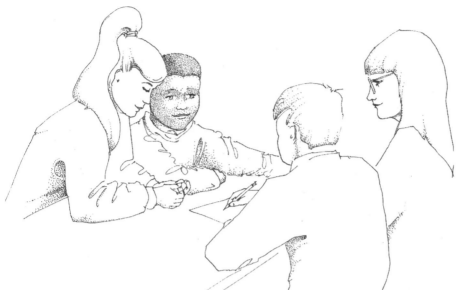

Where do we begin?

As we examine the concept of the learner-centered school, we should remember that different students, different teachers, different schools, and different systems will vary in their rates and in their patterns of learning, acceptance of change, and implementation of new ideas and programs. Changing from the traditional, factory system to the multiage, learner-centered concept involves multiple innovations, changes in educational philosophy, and changes in expectations. Schools, teachers, and systems should begin slowly introducing components to their community and gaining support over time rather than effecting change immediately. It is better to move slowly and effect lasting change than to attempt to revolutionize the school overnight and meet with the resistance that will surely cause the program to fail. Use the following ideas for successful transition to learner-centered classrooms.

IRI/Skylight Publishing, Inc.

Your Ideas

- Visit other classrooms/schools.
- Arrange both your room and your schedule flexibly.
- Set up learning centers.
- Supply concrete materials for hands-on activities.
- Provide a wide variety of trade books.
- Allow for peer tutoring.
- Allow students to have more say in their learning activities.
- Try team teaching with a co-worker.
- Structure the curriculum around themes; integrate the learning.
- Try cooperative learning.
- Encourage independence and responsibility.
- Read, study, and learn as much as you can before you begin.

Shifting to a learner-centered classroom does not have to mean a total changeover. It can be phased in gradually in your classroom or in the entire school. The first step is for you to identify what you and your colleagues do that is learner-centered. Then you will want to consider what you can add.

Changing your classroom

Using the "Now Do—Can Add" charts on the following pages, you can begin moving toward more learner-centered practices.

First, review the practices which contribute to learner-centeredness in the classroom. In the upper half of the chart (do), identify the practices that you already include in your repertoire. You may want to rate each practice on a scale of 1 (sometimes) to 5 (regularly). In the lower half of the chart, identify those learner-centered practices that you could add to your classroom.

Second, identify the barriers to your success in doing more of what you already do or to add practices new to your repertoire. In naming the barriers, do not include time or money.

Third, select the first three changes you are going to make and enter these on the steps.

Finally, give yourself a realistic timeline for introducing and evaluating the new practices.

Your Ideas

Teamwork for change

Making the shift to a learner-centered school may take more time and effort and, certainly, much collaboration. For the next task, join with colleagues to ask and answer certain questions.

First, ask the question, What does it mean to be learner-centered? Use the cardstorming method to answer this question. Ask each person on your team to take index cards or sticky notes and write one-to-three- word descriptions of the attributes each feels to be important. Allow up to ten minutes before each person selects the attribute he or she thinks is most important. Post these on a wall. If items are exactly the same or similar, start to form some columns of like items. After the first set of items are posted, ask each to pick the attribute that will be most difficult to implement. Post these in the columns. Move items to form new columns as the group agrees until you are working with four to eight columns. Continue by having individuals offer the rest of the items and put them in the columns agreed to by the group. After all the attributes are up on the wall, help the group to name the columns. Use the names of the column heading to frame your operational definition of the learner-centered school. "The learner-centered school is a place where. . . ." Allow sixty to ninety minutes for the entire task.

Second, ask the question, How is our school already learner-centered? Using the "Now Do—Can Add" chart for the learner-centered school, have pairs review specific chapters and identify the practices already in existence in your school which contribute to learner-centeredness.

IRI/Skylight Publishing, Inc.

*Your
Ideas*

(Index cards or sticky notes speed the discussion of what should go on the chart.) Rate each selected item on a scale of 1 (a little bit) to 5 (a standard practice throughout the school).

Third, ask, What can we do to make the school more learner- centered? Have pairs work on a different column than they worked on in the above step. From the review and other ideas it sparked, add details for "can do." Encourage wide open brain- storming on the index cards or sticky notes for the "can do" list. In this round, agree only on what column an item fits under on the chart.

Fourth, use the card-storming method to list and name the barriers your team might face in making the school more learner-centered. After the barriers are named, discuss and agree on how far the team wants to go in making the school more learner-centered. Do you want a whole-scale restructuring with major changes in curriculum? instruction? assessment? organization? Or do the barriers tell you it would be more realistic to take smaller steps? What is your realistic goal?

Fifth, ask, What are the most important steps you must take to achieve your schoolwide goal? (Put them in sequence: first, second, third, etc.) What are the timelines for finishing each step? Who will be responsible for the tasks? If your team follows this review, you can establish a plan in less than five hours' time.

Going forward

As you think about going forward with the plan, be sure it includes community involvement, third-party review, time allowance, and assessment.

- Community involvement means making sure that all steps include the concerns of parents, business, and community leaders. Be sure to ask yourself, How will I bring others outside the team into the plan?
- Go outside the planning team and seek third-party review from other educators who can critique your

plan and help ensure that you have considered all options. A local university, professional education association field representatives, colleagues in other districts that have introduced learner-centered education, consultants, and the chamber of commerce can be your resources.

- Allow sufficient time for change. Everything takes longer than expected. As you institute your plan, remember that Rome was not built in a day and neither was a restructured school.

- Assessment is important during change; you cannot review your school's progress too often as it restructures itself. Have a schedule and a strategy to review progress at least once a month. Keep a portfolio of monthly accomplishments and check them against your timelines.

Your Ideas

Becoming More Learner-Centered: What I Can Do in My Classroom

	Curriculum	Instruction	Classroom Organization	Assessment	Parent Involvement	Other
NOW DO						
CAN ADD						

IRI/Skylight Publishing, Inc.

My Barriers to Success

My First Three Steps

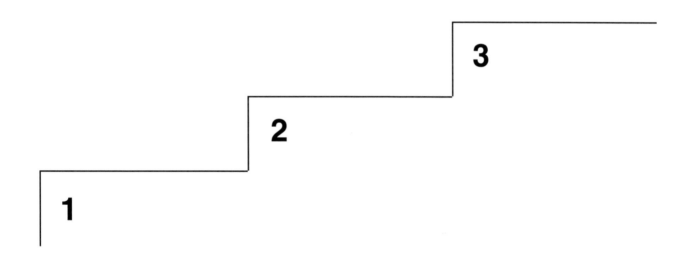

My Timelines For This Year

Today   _____   _____   _____

Becoming More Learner-Centered:
What We Need to Do in Our <u>School</u>

	Curriculum	Instruction	Classroom Organization	Assessment	Parent Involvement	Other
N O W D O						
C A N A D D						

IRI/Skylight Publishing, Inc.

Our Barriers to Success

Our First Three Steps

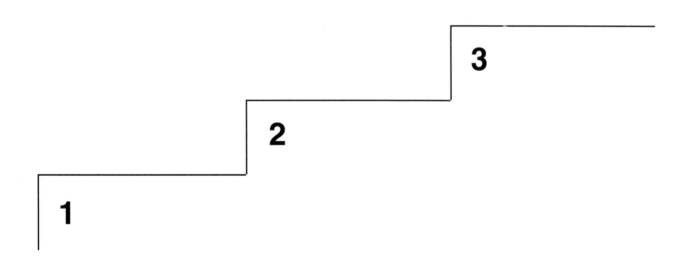

Our Timelines For This Year

Today

IRI/Skylight Publishing, Inc.

Bibliography

Alexander, P. A., & Murphy, P. K. (1993). The research base for APA's learner-centered psychological principles. In B. L. McCombs (Chair), *Taking research on learning seriously: Implications for teacher education,* Invited symposium at the annual meeting of the American Educational Research Association, New Orleans, April 1994.

Ambruster, B., & Anderson, T. (1980). *The effect of mapping on the free recall of expository tests* (Tech. Rep. No. 160). Urbana-Champaign, IL: University of Illinois, Center for the Study of Reading.

Anderson, R. (1993, January). The return of the non-graded classroom. *Principal.*

Anderson, R. (1973). *Opting for openness.* Arlington, VA: National Association of Elementary School Principals.

Archbald, D., & Newmann, F. (1988). *Beyond standardized testing: Assessing authentic academic achievement in the secondary school.* Reston, VA: National Association of Secondary School Principals.

Ausubel, D. (1978). *Educational psychology: A cognitive view* (2nd ed.). New York: Holt, Rinehart and Winston.

Bellanca, J. (1992). *The cooperative think tank II: Graphic organizers to teach thinking in the cooperative classroom.* Palatine, IL: IRI/Skylight Publishing, Inc.

Bellanca, J. (1991). *Building a caring, cooperative classroom.* Palatine, IL: IRI/Skylight Publishing, Inc.

Bellanca, J. (1990). *The cooperative think tank.* Palatine, IL: IRI/Skylight Publishing, Inc.

IRI/Skylight Publishing, Inc.

Bellanca, J.,Chapman, C., & Swartz, E. (1994). *Multiple assessments for multiple intelligences.* Palatine, IL: IRI/Skylight Publishing, Inc.

Bellanca, J., & Fogarty, R. (1991). *Blueprints for thinking in the cooperative classroom* (2nd ed.). Palatine, IL: IRI/Skylight Publishing, Inc.

Bellanca, J., & Fogarty, R. (1986). *Catch them thinking: A handbook of classroom strategies.* Palatine, IL: IRI/Skylight Publishing, Inc.

Bellanca, J., & Swartz, E. (Eds.). (1994). *The challenge of detracking: A collection.* Palatine, IL: IRI/Skylight Publishing, Inc.

Berliner, D., & Casanova, W. (1993). *Putting research to work in your school.* Jefferson City, MO: Scholastic, Inc.

Braddock, II, J. H. (1993). Tracking: Implications for student race-ethnic subgroups. In J. Bellanca and E. Swartz (Eds.) *The challenge of detracking: A collection.* Palatine, IL: IRI/Skylight Publishing, Inc.

Brandt, R. (1992). A fresh focus for curriculum. *Educational Leadership, 49*(8), 78.

Brown, A. Campione, J., & Day, J. (1981). Learning to learn: On training students to learn from texts. *Educational Researcher, 10*(2), 14–21.

Brown, A., & Palincsar, A. (1982). Inducing strategic learning from texts by means of informed, self-control training. *Topics in Learning and Learning Disabilities, 2.*

Burke, K. (1994). *The mindful school: How to assess authentic learning.* Palatine, IL: IRI/Skylight Publishing, Inc.

Campbell, L., Campbell, B., & Dickinson, D. (1992). *Teaching and learning through multiple intelligences.* Seattle, WA: New Horizons for Learning.

Carroll, J. M. (1990). The Copernican plan: Restructuring the American high school. *Phi Delta Kappan, 71*(5), 358–365.

Chapman, C. (1993). *If the shoe fits...: How to develop multiple intelligences in the classroom.* Palatine, IL: IRI/Skylight Publishing, Inc.

Chapman, C., Swartz, E., & Bellanca, J. (1994). *Multiple assessments for multiple intelligences.* Palatine, IL: IRI/Skylight Publishing, Inc.

Cohen, E. (1986). *Designing groupwork: Strategies for the heterogeneous classroom.* New York: Teachers College Press.

Costa, A. (1991). *The school as a home for the mind.* Palatine, IL: IRI/Skylight Publishing, Inc.

Costa, A. (Ed.). (1985). *Developing minds.* Alexandria, VA: Association for Supervision and Curriculum Development.

Costa, A., Bellanca, J., & Fogarty, R. (Eds.). (1992). *If minds matter: A foreword to the future.* Volumes I & II. IRI/Skylight Publishing, Inc.

Dansereau, D., et al. (1979). Development and evaluation of a learning strategy training program. *Journal of Educational Psychology, 71*(1).

Davidson, J. (1982). The group mapping activity for instruction in reading and thinking. *Journal of Reading, 26*(1), 52–56.

Davis, B., et al. (June, 1991). *Continuous progress with multiage grouping and teacher teaming: A nongraded implementation guide for small school districts.* Austin, TX: Texas Education Agency.

de Bono, E. (1983). The direct teaching of thinking as a skill. Phi Delta Kappan, 64(1), 703–708.

Dewey, J. (1916). *Democracy and education: An introduction to the philosophy of education.* New York: The Macmillan Company.

Ferrara, S., & McTighe, J. (1992). Assessment: A thoughtful process. In A. Costa, J. Bellanca, & R. Fogarty (Eds.). *If minds matter: A foreword to the future Vol. II,* pp. 337–348. Palatine, IL: IRI/Skylight Publishing, Inc.

Fogarty, R. (Ed.). (1993). *The multiage classroom: A collection.* Palatine, IL: IRI/Skylight Publishing, Inc.

Fogarty, R. (1994). *The mindful school: How to teach for metacognitive reflection.* Palatine, IL: IRI/Skylight Publishing, Inc.

Fogarty, R. (1991). *The mindful school: How to integrate the curricula.* Palatine, IL: IRI/Skylight Publishing, Inc.

Fogarty, R. (1988). *Start them thinking.* Palatine, IL: IRI/Skylight Publishing, Inc.

Fogarty, R. & Bellanca, J. (1987). *Patterns for thinking: Patterns for transfer.* Palatine, IL: IRI/Skylight Publishing, Inc.

Fogarty, R., Perkins, D., & Barell, J. (1992). *The mindful school: How to teach for transfer.* Palatine, IL: IRI/Skylight Publishing, Inc.

Fullan, M. (1982). *The meaning of educational change.* New York: Teachers College, Columbia University.

Gardner, H. (1991). *The unschooled mind.* U.S.A.: Harper Collins.

Gardner, H. (1987). Developing the spectrum of human intelligences: Teaching in the eighties, a need to change. *Harvard Educational Review, 57,* 187–93.

Gardner, H. (1983). *Frames of mind: The theory of multiple intelligences.* New York: Basic Books.

Gaustad, J. (1991). *Non-age-graded primary schools.* Portland, OR: The Center for Urban Research in Education, Portland State University.

Goldberg, M. F. (1991, September). Portrait of Reuven Feuerstein. *Educational Leadership.*

Goodlad, J., & Anderson, R. (1987). *The nongraded elementary school.* New York: Teachers College Press.

Hall, G., & Hord, S. (1987). *Change in schools: Facilitating the process.* Albany, NY: State University of New York Press.

Hart, L. (1975). *How the brain works: A new understanding of human learning, emotion, and thinking.* New York: Basic Books. Hill, D. (1990, April). Order in the classroom. *Teacher Magazine, 1*(7), 70–77.

Jacobs, H. (Ed.). (1989). *Interdisciplinary curriculum: Design and implementation.* Alexandria, VA: Association for Supervision and Curriculum Development.

Johnson, D., & Johnson, R. (1989). *Leading the cooperative school.* Edina, MN: Interaction Book Company.

Johnson, D., & Johnson, R. (1983). The socialization and achievement crisis: Are cooperative learning experiences the solution? In L. Bickman (Ed.), *Applied Social Psychology Annual 4.* Beverly Hills, CA: Sage Publishing.

Johnson, D., & Johnson, R. (1979). Conflict in the classroom: Controversy and learning. *Review of Educational Research, 49,* 51–70.

Johnson, D., Johnson, R., & Holubec, E. (1988). *Cooperation in the classroom.* Edina, MN: Interaction Book Company.

Johnson, D., Maruyama, G., Johnson, R., Nelson, D., & Skow, L. (1981). Effects of cooperative, competitive, and individualistic goal structures on achievement: A meta-analysis. *Psychological Bulletin, 89,* 47–62.

Johnson, D., & Matross, R. (1977). The interpersonal influence of the psychotherapist. In A. Gurman and A. Razin (Eds.), *The effective therapist: A handbook.* Elmsford, NY: Pergamon Press.

Jones, B. (1987). *Teaching thinking skills.* Washington, D.C.: NEA Professional Library.

Joyce, B., & Showers, B. (1988). *Student achievement through staff development.* White Plains, NY: Longman, Inc.

Joyce, B., & Weil, M. (1986). *Models of teaching.* Englewood Cliffs, NJ: Prentice-Hall.

Katz, L., et al. (1990). *The case for mixed-age grouping in early education.* Washington, DC: National Association for the Education of Young Children.

Kohn, A. (1993). *Punished by rewards: The trouble with gold stars, incentive plans, A's, praise, and other bribes.* New York: Houghton Mifflin.

Marzano, R., & Arredondo, D. (1986, May). Restructuring schools through the teaching of thinking skills. *Educational Leadership, 43*(8), 23.

McTighe, J., & Lyman, F. (1992). Mind tools for matters of the mind. In A. Costa, J. Bellanca, & R. Fogarty (Eds.). *If minds matter: A foreword to the future* Vol. II, pp. 71–90. Palatine, IL: IRI/Skylight Publishing, Inc.

Ministry of Education, Province of British Columbia. (1991). *Supporting learning: Understanding and assessing the progress of children in the primary program. A resource of parents and teachers.* Victoria, BC, Canada: The Ministry.

New York State Education Department. (1991). *A new compact for learning: Improving public elementary, middle, and secondary education results in the 1990s.* Albany, NY: The University of the State of New York.

Oakes, J. (1993). Keeping track, part 2: Curriculum inequality and school reform. In J. Bellanca and E. Swartz (Eds.). *The challenge of detracking: A collection.* Palatine, IL: IRI/Skylight Publishing, Inc.Oakes, J. (1985). *Keeping track: How schools structure inequality.* New Haven: Yale University Press.

Oakes, J., & Lipton, M. (1990). Tracking and ability grouping: A structural barrier to access and achievement. In College Examination Board (Ed.). *Access to knowledge,* pp. 187–204. New York: Editor.

Pavan, B. (1993). The benefits of nongraded schools. In R. Fogarty (Ed.), *The multiage classroom: A collection* (p. 66). Palatine, IL: IRI/Skylight Publishing, Inc.

Pavan, B. (1977). The nongraded elementary school research on academic achievement and mental health. *Texas Tech. Journal of Education, 4*(2).

Pavan, B. (1973, March). Good news: Research on the nongraded elementary school. *Elementary School Journal, 73,* 233–242.

Pavan, B. (1973, February). Nongradedness: One view. *Educational Leadership, 30,* 401–403.

Perkins, D. (1991). *Smart schools: From training memories to educating minds.* New York: The Free Press.

Perkins, D., & Salomon, G. (1988). Teaching for transfer, *Educational Leadership, 46*(1), 22–32.

Perrone, V. (1991). *Expanding student assessment.* Alexandria, VA: ASCD.

Presseisen, B. (1986). *Thinking skills: Research and practice.* Washington, D.C.: NEA Professional Library.

Purkey, W., Graves, W., & Zellner, M. (1970, December). Self-perceptions of pupils in an experimental elementary school. *Elementary School Journal, 71,* 166–171.

Purnell, S., & Hill, P. (1992). *Time for reform.* Santa Monica, CA: RAND.

Raymond, A. (1992, October). Ungraded primaries begin to take over in Kentucky. *Teaching K-8.*

Senge, P. (1990). *The fifth discipline.* New York: Doubleday.

Slavin, R. (1993). Achievement effects of ability grouping in secondary schools: A best-evidence synthesis. In J. Bellanca and E. Swartz (Eds.) *The challenge of detracking: A collection.* Palatine, IL: IRI/Skylight Publishing, Inc.

Slavin, R. (1986). *Using student team learning: The Johns Hopkins learning project.* Baltimore, MD: The Johns Hopkins Team Learning Project Center for Research on Elementary and Middle Schools, Johns Hopkins University.

Slavin, R. (1984). *Research methods in education: A practical guide.* Englewood Cliffs, NJ: Prentice-Hall.

Slavin, R., & Gutiérrez, R. (1992, Winter). Achievement effects of the nongraded elementary school. A best evidence synthesis. *Review of Educational Research, 62*(4), 333–376.

Slavin, R., Karweit, N., & Madden, N. (1989). *Effective programs for students at risk.* Boston: Allyn and Bacon.

Steinberg, A., & Wheelock, A. (1993). After tracking—What? Middle schools find new answers. In J. Bellanca & E. Swartz (Eds.). *The challenge of detracking: A collection.* Palatine, IL: IRI/Skylight Publishing, Inc.

Sternberg, R. (1986). *Intelligence applied: Understanding and increasing your intellectual skills.* San Diego: Harcourt Brace Jovanovich.

Swartz, R. (1991). Structured teaching for critical thinking and reasoning in standard subject area instruction. In J. Voss, D. Perkins, & J. Segal (Eds.), *Informal reasoning and education* (pp. 405–450). Hillsdale, NJ: Lawrence Erlbaum Associates.

Vogel, F., & Bowers, N. (1972, Winter). Pupil behaviors in a multiage nongraded school. *Journal of Experimental Education, 41,* 78-86.

Vygotsky, L. (1986). *Thought and language.* Cambridge, MA: MIT Press.

Whimbey, A. (1975). *Intelligence can be taught.* New York: Innovative Science.

Williams, R. (1992). *Strategies to transform school systems: The leadership edge.* Vancouver, BC, Canada: EduServ, Inc.

Williams, R. B. (1993). *More than 50 ways to build team consensus.* Palatine, IL:IRI/Skylight Publishing, Inc.

Williams, J. R., & Kopp, W. L. (1993, July). Implementation of Instrumental Enrichment and cognitive modifiability in the Taunton Public Schools: A model for systemic implementation in U.S. schools. A paper submitted in partial fulfillment of the Level II trainer certification requirements at Hadassah—Wizo— Canada Research Institute, Israel (43 pages)

Williams, L. V. (1983). *Teaching for the two-sided mind.* New York: Simon & Schuster, Inc.

IRI/Skylight Publishing, Inc.

Index

IRI/Skylight Publishing, Inc.

NOTES

There are
one-story intellects,
two-story intellects, and three-story
intellects with skylights. All fact collectors, who have
no aim beyond their facts, are one-story men. Two-story men compare,
reason, generalize, using the labors of the fact collectors as well as their
own. Three-story men idealize, imagine, predict—
their best illumination comes from
above, through the skylight.

—Oliver Wendell

Holmes